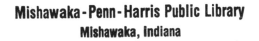

Six Prayers God Always Answers

Tyndale House Publishers, Inc.
Carol Stream, Illinois

Mark Herringshaw &
Jennifer Schuchmann

SIX

prayers

GOD

ALways

ANSWERS*

* Results m

Visit Tyndale's exciting Web site at www.tyndale.com

Six Prayers God Always Answers

Designed by Jacqueline L. Nuñez

Published in association with the literary agency of Alive Communications, Inc., 7680 Goddard Street, Suite 200, Colorado Springs, CO 80920.

Library of Congress Cataloging-in-Publication Data

Herringshaw, Mark.
  Six prayers God always answers / Mark Herringshaw and Jennifer Schuchmann.
    p. cm.
  Includes bibliographical references.
  ISBN-13: 978-1-4143-1867-7 (hc)
  ISBN-10: 1-4143-1867-7 (hc)
1. Prayer—Christianity. I. Schuchmann, Jennifer, date. II. Title.
  BV220.H44 2008
  248.3'2—dc22   2007050575

Printed in the United States of America

14 13 12 11 10 09 08
7   6   5   4   3   2   1

contents

1
Prayer Doesn't Work

Prayer doesn't work.

God works.

We often get that confused, don't we?

We think there is a certain formula we have to follow—a right way of doing prayer. If we do it right, God will answer. It's like using the correct postage after a rate change: the proper stamp ensures delivery. But when our prayers don't get answered, we believe we're somehow at fault. We "prayed the wrong way." There are lots of ways we could have screwed up—not having enough postage (read: good deeds); mislabeling the envelope (praying to Jesus when we should have prayed to God); or forgetting to seal it (with a promise to do better next time).

If that's how you think, this isn't the book for you. We don't believe there's a *right* way or a *wrong* way to pray. Yes, biblical literature, church history, and religious tradition present some great guidelines when we need an example to follow, but the truth is that prayer is nothing more than communication with God. Some of us prefer long, elegantly handwritten notes on premium stationery. Others prefer text messages with abbreviated words that aren't grammatically correct (and that parents can't decipher). But regardless of *how* we pray, it isn't prayer that changes things. *It's God who changes things.*

Sometimes we forget that.

We're so caught up in our own expectations of what prayer should look and smell like that when we look for God's reply, we limit our thinking to a #10 business envelope in the mailbox, when perhaps God is answering us with a marshmallow, an old lady's smile, or something else so completely unexpected that we miss it.

Consider the example of the Sunday school teacher who asked her young students to guess the answer to a question.

"Okay, class, I'm thinking of something brown and fuzzy that jumps from tree to tree. Does anyone know what I'm thinking of?"

No one in the class responded, so she tried again.

"Okay, it has a bushy tail, plays in your yard, and is very hard to catch. Now do you know what I am thinking of?"

Again the kids remained quiet.

Exasperated, the Sunday school teacher gave it one last try.

"Okay, it's a small animal that eats nuts. Does anybody know what I am talking about?"

Finally, Bobby raised his hand.

"Teacher, I know the right answer is Jesus, but it sure sounds like you're talking about a squirrel."

From our earliest experiences at church, we learn that it is more important to be right than to be authentic. So it's no wonder that, when it comes to prayer, we'd rather say the right words, follow the correct formula, and assume the designated posture, even when it feels phony to us.

SET UP FOR FAILURE

Regardless of our competence or success at work, home, or school, and independent of our awards and accolades, we continue to experience situations where we feel out of control. Life brings an endless parade of intense moments of beauty, pain, injustice, confusion, and hopelessness, that takes us past the end of ourselves and leaves us searching for someone or something else.

We never have enough.

It's never good enough.

We continually come up short.

Life is hard, and we often seem ill-equipped for the challenges.

What if this is intentional?

Could it be that we were set up to fail on our own?

What if the Creator of the universe shaped a world that is complicated beyond the comprehension of the people who live there? So complicated that they can't exist in it without crying out for help?

What would that world look like?

It would be a world filled with desperate and needy people.

And everyone would be praying.

ADMIT IT OF NOT—YOU PRAY

Jordan is a typical twelve-year-old American boy: interested in basketball, video games, and text messaging his friends. His life is complicated, and his toys are sophisticated.

While at a friend's house, Jordan discovers a toddler book that captures his attention. The board book contains six magnetic cardboard cars that can be placed on the pages and moved around. Designed as an interactive storybook for toddlers, the toy is lying idly on the table until Jordan finds it. He opens the front cover, takes out the cars, and insists on "testing" the cars on every page in the book.

When Lily, the eleven-year-old girl of the house, catches Jordan playing with her little brother's book, she can't help but comment, "Uh, Jordan, you're playing with a baby toy."

Instead of being embarrassed, Jordan turns to Lily and says, "Oh, you know you play with it, too, when no one else is around."

Her immediate blush and slight smile betray what she won't admit—she plays with her little brother's toys.

And why not? Some things are too irresistible. We may not want to admit it, but prayer is one of those things that a lot of us play around with when no one else is looking. Especially when we're desperate.

When Emily was thirteen, she borrowed a valuable necklace from a friend, intending to return it. When she discovered the necklace was missing, she panicked. First, she tore apart her own room. Then she started through the rest of the house. Eventually, the whole family helped in the search.

Emily was terrified, and rightly so. From behind a

torrent of tears, she cried out, "Help me, God! Where is it?"
She took a breath or two and her face relaxed, reflecting
a strange peace that settled upon her. A thought flashed
through her mind. She ran down the hall to her room,
swung open her closet door, and searched for a particular
pair of forgotten jeans. There in the pocket of her jeans,
she found the necklace.

Those two events—a prayer hurled into the air and a
sudden insight that solved the problem—happened close
enough together that a reasonable person might suppose a
connection, maybe even a genuine cause-and-effect relationship.

Events like these have occurred together so often
throughout history that we have come to believe, in our col-
lective consciousness, that prayer actually makes a difference in the real world. So we pray.

Apparently, we always have.

Prayers From History
Our ancestors scratched their prayers on cavern walls:

> "May the Master of the Buffalo grant us success
>   on our hunt."
> "May the One behind the Clouds send us rain."
> "May the Hand That Moves the Stars lift away my
>   grief."

Many of the architectural wonders built by the great
river-valley civilizations in Egypt, Mesopotamia, India, and
China, and in the mountain and forest city-states of Central
and South America, are religious structures. In those worlds

so distant from our own, human actions were permeated with the scent of prayer.

When the Constitutional Convention of the not-so-united American states convened in Philadelphia in May 1787, the fledgling nation needed a viable government, but few gamblers would have wagered that the feuding former colonies would ever forge a "United States of America."

A heated debate raged for weeks. Part of the New York delegation had already departed for home. Others were preparing to follow. At a crucial moment, an aged Ben Franklin tottered to his feet. Franklin, at that time, was the most distinguished and accomplished living American. Though a Deist steeped in the Enlightenment, who espoused an impassible separation between God and the physical world, Franklin roused his squabbling fellow delegates with the following appeal:

> In the beginning of the contest with G. Britain, when we were sensible of danger we had daily prayer in this room for the Divine Protection. Our prayers, Sir, were heard, and they were graciously answered. All of us who were engaged in the struggle must have observed frequent instances of a Superintending providence in our favor. . . . And have we now forgotten that powerful friend? or do we imagine that we no longer need His assistance. . . .
>
> The longer I live, the more convincing proofs I see of this truth—that God governs in the affairs of men. And if a sparrow cannot fall to the ground without his notice, is it probable that an empire can rise without his aid? We have been assured, Sir, in the sacred writ-

ings that "except the Lord build they labor in vain that build it.". . .

I therefore beg leave to move—that henceforth prayers imploring the assistance of Heaven, and its blessings on our deliberations, be held in this Assembly every morning before we proceed to business.[1]

Almost immediately, the Convention turned a corner. In the following days, the delegates crafted history's most original and enduring outline for human government: the Constitution of the United States of America and its first ten amendments, the Bill of Rights.

Serious and not-so-serious students of history now disagree over the religious beliefs our Founding Fathers once held. But the reasonable proximity of the events must be noted alongside the incongruity and irony of this scene. Ben Franklin, champion for scientific empiricism and a skeptic of anything "spiritual," credited shifts of history to the supernatural intervention of God. He then pleaded with his colleagues to pray for a solution to their impasse.

Constitutions from conflict.

Word pictures on the walls of caves.

Necklaces from forgotten jeans.

Languages

We talk to God, but we don't all speak the same language. One person's prayer comes wrapped in a work of art, like Fabriano's *Nativity*, Handel's *Messiah*, or little Jimmy's finger painting, *Jesus Raises Stinking Lazarus*.

Another prayer might appear as a dramatic enactment, such as the Jewish Passover or a Native American rain

7

dance. Prayer might waft above a city, sung from atop a mosque tower. It might tumble from the lips of a sniffling child, meander along the lyrics of a Kentucky bluegrass song, or conceal itself in the eloquent silence of a Benedictine friar.

Communicating with God takes many forms in its effort to express our common predicament. Our reach is never long enough, our fingers never nimble enough. We run out of time, stamina, and will. Our ambitions outpace our capacity, and the gap cannot be spanned by noble savagery or advanced technology.

And then?

We kneel down. We look up.

And when we don't get the response we're expecting, we look inside ourselves and ask, "What did I do wrong?"

WHaT prayer IS NOT
It is said that St. Catherine's Monastery near Mount Sinai, Egypt, still honors the final will and testament of three monks who lived there twelve centuries ago. One monk, who was a doorkeeper, wanted to keep his job forever. In honor of his request, his mummy still sits beside the door he guarded when he was alive.

Behind that door lived the other two monks. Each had taken a vow to devote his life to perpetual prayer. One would pray while the other slept. They never spoke to or saw each other. Their only connection was a chain that ran through the wall and was attached to their wrists. When one had completed his prayers, he would yank the chain as a signal for the other to begin.

When the two men died, their skeletons were laid side by

side in caskets. And there they rest today, still united by the same chain.[2]

Some historians believe that rigorous monastic disciplines like the one practiced by these two monks helped to preserve civilization during the cultural deterioration of the early Middle Ages.

Perhaps.

But anecdotes like these, told as sermon illustrations by well-intentioned pastors, may unintentionally decrease not only the occurrence of prayer but also the number of active pray-ers. When the average twenty-first-century Westerner hears of such eccentric dedication, a typical response might be, "If this is what it takes to pray to God, count me out."

Prayer isn't accomplished by some divine formula. Its power isn't amplified if we assume some sort of ascetic or monastic posture.

Religion has a way of complicating prayer, making it self-conscious, rehearsed, and . . . well, awkward. We found through some informal research that although nearly everyone in church feels comfortable requesting prayer aloud in a small group, nearly eight out of ten feel uncomfortable actually praying aloud. In other words, 80 percent of the people we surveyed had no problem verbalizing their requests to a pastor, teacher, or small-group leader—even in front of their peers. But they became physically uncomfortable when asked to verbalize their prayers directly to God when others were listening.

Well-meaning prayer tutors often respond to this issue by teaching acronyms such as A.C.T.S. (Adoration, Confession, Thanksgiving, and Supplication) as a way of remembering what to include in a prayer. But the result is that we get

9

hung up on the steps. *Did I spend long enough on the A? And do I really need more T before I can get to the S? How much C?* They seem to emphasize style over substance. Prayer techniques meant to teach us to look up often have the unintended consequence of making us look over our shoulders. *Am I doing this right?*

Prayer isn't work. Or at least it shouldn't be.

Prayer should be like communicating with a lover.

Sometimes words aren't necessary.

Regardless of what the magazines teach, a good kiss doesn't happen from good technique. It's not about how warm, moist, and soft—if so, we'd all be kissing cinnamon rolls.

It's not the how but the who.

Prayer, like a kiss, is best when it's about the *other person*.

Especially if the other person is God.

WHAT Prayer Is

Prayer is a conversation with God.

Real prayer has the same elements as a real conversation—bold questions, bursts of emotion, and room for silence. Think of the times when you've had a real, honest-to-goodness conversation with someone you love. It can happen at any time—when your teenager comes home from school, over the dinner table, in bed with your spouse, or in the middle of the night when your toddler wakes up from a nightmare. Conversation isn't rehearsed; it just bursts forth as a response to the situation.

Ellie bounces into the kitchen, where her mom and dad are finishing their dinner. "Can I go to a friend's house tonight and take the car?"

"Whose house?" asks her mother.

"What time will you be home?" asks her father.

"I'm just going to Sarah's. I'll be home by ten."

"Is anyone else going with you?" asks Mom.

"No, just me, but Cindy's meeting us there."

"Is there gas in the car?" asks Dad.

"I'll check," she says and runs out the door. A few minutes later, she's back in the kitchen with a report that the gauge is almost on *E*.

Her dad hands her some cash, tells her he loves her, and reminds her to drive carefully.

There is no formal presentation to this encounter. Nobody carefully planned their words. Ellie, in a hurry to get to her friend's house, asked the most direct question she could. Everything else that took place in the exchange was a result of that first question.

Ellie's conversation wasn't self-conscious or insecure. Prayer shouldn't be either.

We don't carefully calculate our words into some sort of exploitative formula; instead, we're focused entirely on the person to whom we're speaking—to their responses, as well as our own.

Good prayer is like talking with children. We're more interested in hearing what they've said, or how they're reacting to what we've said, than we are in carefully selecting our words.

Sometimes prayer means we get naked—as with sexual intimacy—revealing parts of ourselves that no one else has ever seen. The only reason we can do this is not that the lights are turned off, but because there is trust in the relationship.

God doesn't ask us to undress in front of him, and then go off and share the details with his buddies. He doesn't betray us, even when we've shown him *everything*. Prayer, like a comfortable, intimate conversation, is a safe place to be vulnerable. And whether or not we get enough A and C before our T or S, God will still be there in the morning.

Prayer is instinctual

Prayer can and does flow deliberately from discipline or habit, but it can also burst forth instinctively. Often the most precious prayers don't look like prayers at all. They come out unbidden. They accidentally rupture, impulsively burst out, or covertly distance themselves. They are buried in our unfiltered reactions to the joys and pains and fears of typical days in typical lives. If such prayers could find a voice of their own, we might not even realize they were prayers at all. They sound unassuming, unpretentious, brash, down-to-earth, and often shockingly irreverent.

A near miss at a busy intersection and someone screams, "Oh, my god."

An employer breaks a promise and the victim mutters, "Oh, my god."

A patient hears a medical report, covers her mouth, and weeps, "Oh, my god."

A soldier deployed in the desert holds a perfumed letter and pounds his helmet against a concrete wall, venting, "Oh, my god."

It is hardly an exaggeration to call prayer an instinct. Before we think, consider the implications, weigh the probabilities, or balance our philosophic algebra, we pray.

Following the terrorist attacks of 9/11, many New

Yorkers found themselves in the throes of two indulgences most would have resisted in less-complicated times. Hundreds threw themselves into sexual encounters with total strangers, and thousands lost themselves in public displays of prayer.[3] Here's how Peggy Noonan described the instinct to pray in her *Wall Street Journal* column on September 28, 2001:

> In the past 17 days, since the big terrible thing, our country has, unconsciously but quite clearly, chosen a new national anthem. It is "God Bless America," the song everyone sang in the days after the blasts to show they loved their country. It's what they sang on television, it's what kids sang in school, it's what families sang in New York at 7 p.m. the Friday after the atrocity, when we all went outside with our candles and stood together in little groups in front of big apartment buildings. A friend of mine told me you could hear it on Park Avenue from uptown to downtown, the soft choruses wafting from block to block.

There is comfort in the touch of others . . . and in the touch of Another.

Consider the explosive growth, through the last half of the twentieth century, of the practice of Christian prayer in atheist China. Defying bitter opposition from a thoroughly secular Communist government, somewhere between 50 million and 100 million people in China privately but regularly practice some form of Christian intercession.[4]

Spiritual connection is an unquenchable, untamable human drive. Civil institutions may attempt to forbid it.

Religious institutions may attempt to regulate it. But prayer, one of the most intimately personal and democratic of human impulses, thrives.

And it always will thrive, because prayer rises from the deepest wells in the human soul: the desperate awareness that we are inadequate to manage the challenges of our own lives.

Alone in his suburban Minneapolis house, Jay saw flames. Despite his certainty that everyone else was gone, he yelled, "Fire!" He recognized the stupidity of it the moment he opened his mouth, yet he continued to yell "Fire!" to the empty house. Unbeknownst to him, his daughter was in the basement. Had Jay not yelled—despite his conviction that no one was in the house—it is likely she would have died.

Some may be certain there is no God. And if there is, he is hands-off. He doesn't hear us. And he doesn't answer our prayers. Yet we still call out to him. We toss up prayers like we toss up a rubber ball.

But what if there were real meaning behind our throw-away words?

What if these casual words we speak are actually sacred?

What if our prayer promptings are not only *to* God, but also *from* God?

OH, MY GOD

Two college girls were in the hallway talking about the night before. One sipped her overpriced latte while the other waved her Diet Coke in a dramatic retelling of a conversation with her boyfriend.

"When he found out, he was like, 'Oh, my god,' and I was like, 'Oh, my god.'"

For most of us, our only thought about such a situation would be how to walk past the speaker without, like, getting sprayed from, like, an overflow of soda, should, like, her gesticulations get any more boisterous. But when Billy walked past this very conversation, he heard something that most of us wouldn't.

A poem.

Specifically, a haiku.

Haiku originated in Japan in the nineteenth century and were traditionally about nature. Today, a haiku can cover any subject, as long as it follows the general form of seventeen syllables arranged in three lines in a 5-7-5 pattern. Overhearing the girl's words, Billy immediately formatted the casual conversation into a poetic expression:

> *When he found out he*
> *was like oh my god and I*
> *was like oh my god*[5]

Why did Billy hear a poetic recitation while the rest of us only heard mind-numbing girl talk?

Perhaps it is because Billy Collins is a former poet laureate of the United States. He spends his days writing and rewriting words into verse. He's trained, skilled, and experienced in writing poetry, in plucking phrases out of conversation and turning them into art. The speaker didn't know her words were poetry, or that she was creating literary art. She didn't recognize anything interesting in her language pattern, her choice of words, or her arrangement of syllables. She was just, like, telling a story.

What if it hadn't been Billy Collins who walked by the girls that day? What if it had been, say, Billy Graham? Graham has had a different kind of education and training. What would he have recognized in the casual words of the girls' conversation?

Put another way, what if a person trained, skilled, and experienced in prayer had walked by?

Instead of a poem, would he have heard a prayer?

Would a pray-er laureate have recognized the girl's words as a plea for relationship with a God outside of herself? Would he have understood her need for a *personal* deity as expressed in her words "*my* god"?

Life is tough and we are hopeful. We simultaneously accept our lot and search for ways to improve it. But what if our answer were found in the very words we are most likely to throw away?

The girl in the hallway knows that life is shocking. She knows that some circumstances are too hard to handle on her own, yet like all of us, she presses on, constantly seeking solutions to ease her burdens. What if the solution to her problems were in the words she so thoughtlessly tossed up in the hallway?

There are certain situations that prompt us to pray.

1. **Bargaining Prayers.** We get pulled over for a speeding ticket, and we pray for a warning and promise never to speed again; or our bank account is low, and we promise that if the check doesn't bounce we won't overspend again. "Please God, just this once. I promise I won't do it again."

2. **Questioning Prayers.** When we're alone and lonely,

we want to know whether anyone else is there, whether anyone cares. "God, are you there?"

3. **Prayers for Justice.** When we see injustice in the world, we pray for things we want less of, such as war, betrayal, abuse, kidnappings, and slavery. We call out in frustration, "God, it's so unfair!"

4. **Desperate Prayers.** When we're desperate, we don't even stop to ask if God is there; we simply believe it because there is nothing else to believe. We're so desperate that we can't do it on our own, and we know it. "God, please don't let her die."

5. **Audacious Prayers.** When we're so preoccupied with ourselves and our needs, we pray selfish prayers. "God, please let me win the lottery."

6. **Prayers of Beauty and Happiness.** When we see great beauty or experience great joy (the taste of a fine wine or chocolate, great sex, a first kiss, a bride floating down the aisle in a cloud of white), we want more, and so we pray, "Oh, God, I want more. Please let me experience this again."

It seems our prayers well up around the things we love—a child, a spouse's beauty, our own lives—and things we fear, notably, the fear of losing what we love.

Consider these expressions that we hear around us all the time:

"God, help me. I'll never do it again."
"God, are you there?"
"Goddamn it!"
"Save me, God!"

"Please, God!"
"Oh, god, you're beautiful."

Whether on TV, in the movies, or in conversation, people thoughtlessly invoke the name of God into the mundane ("Oh, my God!") and the profane ("Jesus Christ!"). Believers are offended—convinced it is disrespectful, even blasphemous. Nonbelievers toss it up to a slip of the tongue ("Pardon my French") or simply give it no thought at all.

But what if these were really prayers?

Oh, sure, they're not the kind of prayers found in a Baptist Sunday school class or at a Catholic Mass; they aren't led by a Lutheran minister or a Jewish rabbi.

Tim, a recent seminary graduate hoping to start his own church, asked, "Does a father stop listening to his child because the kid is swearing at him? Or is he able to see beyond the pain and the hurt that life has inflicted, to see it as a cry of a beloved child, wounded, crying out to Abba? Could Jesus see these outbursts as a cry of a wounded brother or sister? How do we know what is in the heart of those who utter such words? Do we even know our own hearts? We might just be condemning the prayers of a hurting child who is crying out, 'Lord forgive me.'"

God is the judge of these prayers.

And we believe God answers every one of them.

We pray.

God answers.

In the answers, we learn who he is.

2
THE TRADING FLOOR OF THE CHICAGO MERCANTILE EXCHANGE
Bargaining Prayers

DOES GOD NEGOTIATE?

Does he allow us to bargain with him?

Can we trade a few weeks of church attendance for passing a test, or could we get a warning instead of a speeding ticket if we donated to charity?

Is trade with God as lopsided as the rich man found when he tried to take his wealth to heaven? The man packed a suitcase of gold bricks, but when St. Peter met him at the Pearly Gates, he took one look and said, "You brought *pavement*?"

This is the situation many find themselves in when they want to make a deal with God. What are his terms? What is the currency of heaven? Does he take cash or credit? Is he a willing negotiator or the ultimate haggler? Does he strike bargains or just strike them down? Making a deal with God often feels like a blind auction. We want to bid enough to win the prize, but we certainly don't want to overbid.

Whether or not God is a shrewd bargainer, we act as if he is. Forget the images of heaven as a tranquil place of harps and soothing voices. From this side of eternity, heaven's door sounds like the trading floor of the Chicago Mercantile Exchange:

> "God, if I can just close this deal, I will build that orphanage in Africa."
> "Please God, if you send her back, this time I will go to counseling. I promise."
> "If you will let the pregnancy test be negative just this once, I'll never even kiss him again!"

Most of us try bargaining with God. The offers drift skyward by the billions. Prayer is shrewd business. But are we to blame? After all, God started it. He said, "Ask and it will be given to you."[1] And Jesus actually said, "You can ask for anything in my name, and I will do it."[2]

Ask.

So we do.

But what are the rules in this foreign kingdom?

Is asking really enough?

We're not sure. So instead of a straight-up request, many of our prayers arrive on God's dispatch desk with an if/then rider attached. *If* we sweeten the pot, *then* maybe our offers will be accepted more quickly or completely. We are instinctive hagglers, and we can't resist the temptation to stack the odds by strapping on a promise or two:

"If you'll keep my parents from finding out about
Saturday night, I swear I'll tell them the truth about
the car."

"If this tumor is benign, I'll never look at another
XXX-rated Web site again."

"Oh, Jesus, save my baby, and I will do whatever
you ask!"

We hope that God, the first-rate car dealer we imagine
him to be, might take our offers, or at least counter with his
own conditions: "Throw in a week of fasting and a year-end
gift to United Way, and you've got a deal!"

In the absence of knowing the rules, we invent our own.

Most of us have had some experience with prayers that
were answered—our requests were fulfilled immediately
and completely. These fortunate occurrences encourage us
to ask again. But there are other answers to prayer that are
more troubling. Our requests come back partially filled, and
we wait to see if the rest is on back order, or if the part is
no longer available. Occasionally, we see that our prayers
are answered differently from our expectations. Other
requests come back as a resounding no, which technically
is an answer, but it often feels as empty as no answer at
all. This leaves us pondering the rules of trade in this
foreign country.

So we rely on what we know best; we assume the system
is market driven. After all, God has unlimited resources. We
do not. God wishes certain actions from us. We've willfully
withheld them. Seizing the imbalance, we offer God what
we imagine he wants—our obedience—in exchange for
resources out of our reach. Until the Kingdom comes to

earth, why not apply earthly ways when appealing to the Kingdom?

How do you bargain with the unknown?

Perhaps it is the same way you bargain with the known.

These three rules of haggling apply in almost any situation:

1. *Bring cash.* Whether they carry the local currency or American dollars, travelers with cash are often dealt with more favorably than those who want to use credit.
2. *Talk to the owner.* The person who stands to gain or lose the most is the one most willing to make the deal.
3. *Be willing to walk away.* According to experts, this is the most important thing to know. If the sellers know you want the product at any price, they're less likely to offer you favorable terms. But if they think you might walk away and they could lose the deal, it's in their best interest to bargain.

If these principles work on earth, why not in heaven?

It's capitalism at its loftiest, with Adam Smith scribing the ledger in the Book of Life.

BarGainInG WITH GOD

After a series of heart surgeries, Miriam's mother was once again having problems. A bout of bronchitis and a surge of medicines left her dizzy and confused. One night, while Miriam was asleep, her mother got out of bed and fell. She couldn't get up, so she slept on the floor the rest of the night. When Miriam found her mother beside the bed the next morning, she realized how serious the situation was and immediately took her to the emergency room. Miriam shares her experience with prayer during that time:

> As I listened to my mother's labored breathing at the hospital, I prayed. I'm a reasonably observant Jew, and prayer is my habit. But generally my petitions are constructed so that they don't require a material answer. Having learned early that God does not necessarily give you the shiny red bicycle you asked for, I've come to request things that, with a little help, I can find within myself—strength, courage, wisdom.
>
> But this time, I asked for something only God could give me. "Don't," I pleaded, "do this to me. It's one month before my son's bar mitzvah. Don't take her from me now."
>
> My father had died just three years earlier. I could not bear the idea that neither of my parents would be there to see the tradition they had nurtured in me pass to the next generation. "God," I said, "surely You want her to be there."
>
> In the years since, I've realized two things about that prayer. First, it was a sort of bargain. It wasn't quite like the deal a child might try to strike with God: "Don't let the teacher collect the homework today, and I promise I'll do all next week's assignments early." There was, however, a price for what I'd asked.
>
> My mother did recover from the bronchitis, and she made it to my son's bar mitzvah. But she did not have an easy death. Had she succumbed to the upper-respiratory infection, she would have passed away

quickly. Instead, she struggled for another six months with episodes of gasping that came more and more frequently, with deteriorating mobility, with memory lapses, with the thousand indignities of invalid life.[3]

Miriam bargained, but it seemed she got more than she bargained for. In exchange for her mother beaming in the front row at her son's bar mitzvah, Miriam appears to have gotten a front-row seat to her mother's long and painful death. Though Miriam called it a bargain, she didn't explicitly offer up a lengthy and painful death of her mother in exchange for a front-row mother at the bar mitzvah. Instead, she pleaded with a blank check, and it seems that God filled in the amount.

Is that the kind of bargain God makes?

ABRAHAM LINCOLN'S BARGAIN

History shows that even the smartest and most powerful among us resort to bargaining once all other solutions are exhausted. And this kind of appeal to God isn't limited to professing Christians.

Abraham Lincoln was something of an agnostic when he took the presidential oath of office in 1861. But the following autumn, he resorted to bargaining with God. The president had something he knew God wanted, and God had something Lincoln wanted. They made a pact on September 12, and the result seems to have made a believer of Lincoln.

Since the election and the subsequent outbreak of war in 1861, abolitionists had lobbied Lincoln to free the slaves. Though he personally abhorred slavery, he had resisted this pressure, claiming his single purpose was to preserve the

Union. Abolition, he feared, would jeopardize support for the Union in border states like Maryland. Ending slavery might win him the moral high ground, but it might cost him the war. Lincoln stubbornly refused.

But as the bloody months rolled on, with defeat following horrendous defeat at Shiloh, Wilson's Creek, and Bull Run, Lincoln privately began to question whether God was pushing him toward abolition. Just weeks earlier, Robert E. Lee had won a second stunning victory at Manassas, Virginia. Lee then dashed north across the Potomac into Maryland, just seventy miles west of Washington, D.C. Lincoln faced the prospect of losing Maryland to the rebels.

By mid-September, with the defiant rebels now north of the Potomac River, Lincoln yielded—with an offer for God.

The result from God's side appears to have been General George McClellan's bumbling, if not improbable, victory at Antietam, a battle that forced the Confederates out of Maryland. The cost was unimaginable—26,000 Americans lost their lives on that single bloodiest day in U.S. history—but it was the victory for which Lincoln had prayed.

On September 22, 1862, just five days after the battle of Antietam, he told his story and made the announcement that would forever change history.

At noon, he called a meeting with his Cabinet, which included, among others, Salmon Chase, secretary of the treasury, who recorded Lincoln's words in his diary.

"When the rebel army was at Frederick," Lincoln said, "I determined, as soon as it should be driven out of Maryland, to issue a Proclamation of Emancipation such as I thought most likely to be useful. I said nothing to any one; but I made the promise to myself and (hesitating a little)—to my

Maker. The rebel army is now driven out, and I am going to
fulfill that promise."[4]

Lincoln affirmed he was not seeking counsel in this decision. The deal had been struck. He then read the proclamation, which says, in part, "All persons held as slaves within
any State or designated part of a State, the people whereof
shall then be in rebellion against the United States, shall be
then, thenceforward, and forever free."[5]

Unlike Miriam, Abraham Lincoln clearly offered a tit-for-tat
to God. Was McClellan's dubious and costly victory actually
God's concession? Maybe. Maybe not. But Lincoln wasn't
taking any chances. He kept his promise.

THaT'S NOT FaIr!

The Academy Award–winning film *Amadeus* admittedly
extrapolates history in order to highlight the tragedy center-
ing on the eighteenth-century European composers Antonio
Salieri and Wolfgang Amadeus Mozart.

As a boy, Salieri, a devout Catholic, struck a bargain with
God: "Make me a composer," he said, "and I will worship
you through music." Miraculously, the mediocre Salieri rose
in prominence to become the court composer for Emperor
Joseph II in Vienna. He considered his ascent a sign that
God had rewarded his sanctity.

Then Mozart came to Vienna. The young genius was
everything Salieri was not: irreverent, flamboyant, flirta-
tious, and magically gifted. As Mozart's star rocketed
heavenward, Salieri grew jealous and bitterly resentful. The
impious prodigy had paid no religious price for his marvel-
ous gifts. For Salieri, Mozart's gift was the harshest of judgments. Though God had honored his side of their bargain, it

seemed he had made a separate bargain with Mozart—with more favorable terms. From Salieri's vantage point, God had capriciously bestowed talent on an undeserving lecher.

Lisa, a storyteller through the medium of film, feels a similar frustration to Salieri's. It wasn't her desire to become a screenwriter, but she was obedient in responding to the call. "He called me into this," she said, pointing upward.

After accepting this call from God, she enjoyed some initial success in her writing and assumed that future success would come quickly and easily. It didn't. For nearly ten years, she's struggled to find the elusive path that once seemed so certain. Now, Lisa is angry with God that it's taking so long.

"Not only did he dangle a carrot in front of me, he waved it back and forth in front of my face," she said. "Then, he didn't just take the carrot away, no, he *threw* it away. And fed it to another bunny. And the other bunny is an *ugly* one. A big, ugly *gray* one. With white ears! And he's eating *my* carrot!"

Lisa's implied bargain with God was that he would reward her with success if she was obedient. She believed her initial success was a confirmation of the bargain. But as she watched other writers who were lower on the talent pole rise above her on the success ladder, she began to question whether God had come through with his part of the deal.

It's an old story—thinking that God gave someone else what you deserve. An ancient storyteller tells the tale of a landowner who early one morning made a deal with some laborers to work in his fields for the day. Later that afternoon, the owner decided to hire more workers. At the end of the day, when all the laborers lined up to receive their wages, to everyone's surprise, the landowner paid every worker—late arrivals included—the same full-day's wage. Those hired late in the day were, of course, delighted with the man's generosity. But those who were hired first were indignant.

"Why should those who came last receive the same reward?"

To them, the landowner's generosity was anything but fair. Yet he remained unmoved.

"What do you care what I do with my money?" he scolded them. "I kept my deal with you. You have no complaint with me. If I want to be benevolent, what is that to you?"[6]

The landowner kept his bargain with the original workers. But the storyteller was trying to make the point that the landowner was still free to make a new and different bargain with others. Considering that the storyteller was Jesus, it's not hard to imagine that the landowner he referred to is God. Perhaps he was trying to explain how God's "new bargain" was coming to fruition. Rather than the works-based mentality of the ancient Israelites, Jesus was presenting the new deal for those who had spent years walking in the wilderness, sacrificing animals to atone for their sins, and working to earn God's favor. It is likely that the story of this bargain had several layers of meaning.

Perhaps if Jesus were speaking at a different time and place he would have used a different story, one that had context and meaning to that time and place. Maybe he would have said to Salieri, "So what, Antonio, if I want to bestow talent on Mozart?" Or to Lisa he might have said, "What do you care if I give success to another writer?"

Though the example or story would be contextual, the words would be timeless. "What is it to you? I can make an agreement with whomever I please, but my promises to you will always be fulfilled."

BLIND BARGAINING

Charlotte had already spent nine years of her life with morning sickness. The last thing she wanted was another child. But in 1933, women didn't often have the courage to resist their husband's advances. "We live next to a train track," Sam boasted to his poker buddies. "It comes by at 5:00 a.m.—too late to go back to sleep and too early to get up."

Her thirteenth baby was due the third week of April 1934. Charlotte, still grieving the loss of her twelfth—a baby girl—dreaded this birth, as well as the months of indentured service that would follow. Under her stoic German veneer, she began to resent the only one who couldn't resent her back—the fragile life growing in her womb.

The moment her contractions began, Charlotte called for the doctor and by force of habit made her way to the back bedroom of the farmhouse. Her babies came slowly, violently, and large. She braced herself. As the hours passed and the pain increased, her nine-month vigil of bitterness exploded into rage at what this child was doing to her—and would continue to do. In the course of her heavy labor, she closed her eyes, clenched her teeth, and vowed, "I'll never set eyes on it!"

Between contractions, Charlotte lay still and opened her eyes. All she could see was darkness. She closed and opened her eyes again. Nothing.

"My eyes!" She sat up and rubbed them. "I can't see!"

The doctor steadied her shoulders and eased her down onto her pillow.

"It's all right," he said. "You're going to be fine."

He was confident that she would be okay. He had heard of such things—temporary blindness caused by trauma—but after twelve successful deliveries, he hadn't expected such a complication with Charlotte.

The child arrived, healthy and strong. "Well, Lottie, no surprise here," the doctor said. "It's a boy." He paused and thought a moment. "That's nine boys, and two girls living?"

"Take it out," Charlotte moaned.

The doctor ignored her. "He's a big one, Lottie, twelve pounds."

"Get it out of here."

He looked at her anxiously. Then he nodded to the nurse, who wrapped the infant in a blanket and hurried out of the room. Charlotte was clearly not in a state of mind to care for the child.

"Relax. All you need is a little rest," the doctor assured her. "Your vision will return in a few minutes."

But minutes passed into hours. As Charlotte lay in her own dark world, she heard the baby cry in the distance.

"God," she murmured, "help me."

Charlotte had never been particularly religious. Sam, for his part, had attended revival meetings from time to time and had even entertained thoughts of going into ministry. But the church had shunned them both when they had been forced to marry in their teens. Neither had much practice in prayer.

"God," whispered Charlotte, "if you give me my sight, I will give you my life. I'll raise this baby. And I will give him to you."

An hour passed.

When the child cried again, he did more than just wake Charlotte from her sleep—he stirred her maternal heart. She called for the nurse and asked for her baby. The nurse placed the little boy on Charlotte's swollen belly, and she pulled him up and allowed him to nurse. Suddenly, the familiar tenderness coursed through her.

Another hour passed. Gradually, gray shadows began to soften the darkness. In another hour, she could make out shapes and movements and the thick curls on the head of the sleeping child.

Within a few more hours, her sight was fully restored.

Charlotte kept her word. She named the baby Howard and tried to raise him in a way that honored her promise, but she kept her bargain with God a secret. Thirty-five years later, just before she died, she confided the details of her deal with God to her daughter-in-law Joyce—Howard's wife.

Did God make a deal with Charlotte? Perhaps it is just a coincidence that Charlotte's son Howard became a pastor. Howard also had a son who entered the pastorate. Now, seventy-five years later, that son, Mark, is writing about his grandmother's bargain with God.

LIFE-AND-DEATH BARGAINS

Wendell Lawson, the character played by Burt Reynolds in the 1978 film *The End*, learns he has only six months to live. Not wanting to suffer through his final days, he decides to commit suicide—with the help of a delusional mental patient played by Dom DeLuise.

After several failed efforts, Lawson proves to be unbelievably inept at self-destruction. Finally, he swims out to sea in an attempt to drown himself. But there, in a surge of seawater and self-awareness, he realizes he wants to live—regardless of the cost. He begins to bargain with God as he swims back toward shore. His offers are extravagant, such as promising 80 percent of his income to God.

The closer Lawson gets to land, the more he realizes he might in fact survive the ordeal. As his odds continue to improve, his negotiations begin to change. Little by little, he lowers the percentage of his donations until he stumbles ashore, at which time he has whittled down his offer to a fraction of his original vow.

The fleeting durability of impulsive piety is self-evident. Once the pressure wanes, we want to dismiss the bargain— or at least to renegotiate terms. What does God do when we renege on a promise?

In 1969, Philip Salois promised God that if he survived a search-and-rescue mission in the jungles of Vietnam, he would dedicate his life to God's service. Salois did survive the exploit, winning the Silver Star for his heroism. But under the pressure of post-traumatic stress, he blanked out most of the details of the quest, including his comprehensive promise to God.

Five years later, Salois had returned to the States and was working as an insurance broker when he suddenly felt compelled to become a Catholic priest. He left his job in the insurance industry and entered seminary. After ordination, he eventually became national chaplain of the Vietnam Veterans of America.

"It's important to note," Salois says, "that I did not enter the seminary under the duress of that prayer. I entered freely because I discerned that it was where God was calling me. Only after I decided to become a priest did that prayer come back to me."[7]

Evidently, God had taken Salois at his word and had, in his own good time, "called the loan," though Salois had no conscious awareness that he was ever in debt.

STALLING TACTICS

In her groundbreaking 1969 book, *On Death and Dying*, Elisabeth Kubler-Ross observes that people faced with terminal illness move through a series of stages before finally accepting their fate. Kubler-Ross says our impulse to bargain with God has a psychological explanation. She claims that haggling is a delay tactic, just one stage in the whole grief process. Terminally ill patients are shocked, they deny the facts, they're angry, and then they try to bargain their way out. Finally, there is depression as they realize and then accept the inevitable.

Bargaining, according to Kubler-Ross, doesn't change our circumstances. It buys time by triggering one of our brain's clever deceptions, giving us latitude to work our way through despair. While those who take prayer seriously believe that prayer moves God's hand, in Kubler-Ross's world, God transacts no real business in the bargain. It's all a clever mind game.

Could Kubler-Ross be right?

Is bargaining a way for us to buy time?

THE ORIGINAL NEGOTIATION

Haggling with God isn't a twenty-first-century invention; it's actually an ancient practice. The first recorded negotiation between man and God is found in the book of Genesis, and it appears that God does more listening than dealing.

God reveals a secret to Abraham: He is about to destroy the decadent cities, Sodom and Gomorrah. At the time, Abraham's nephew Lot and his family were living in Sodom. Abraham wants to secure their safety, so he begins to dicker with God.

"If there are fifty righteous in the city, will you spare it?"

God concedes. "If there are fifty, I will not destroy it."

"How about forty-five?"

"I'll spare it for forty-five," God says.

"How about forty?"

"Yes, for forty."

"Thirty? Twenty?"

"Yes, if there are as few as twenty righteous, I will spare Sodom."

"Can I speak once more? Can I press you further? How about ten?"

"For the sake of ten I will not destroy the city," God concedes.

But there the bargaining stops. Abraham doesn't push further. God will not relent. As it turns out, there are not ten righteous in Sodom. Only Lot, his wife, and their two daughters escape.[8]

God knew there was only one righteous man; Abraham did not. So did Abraham's participation in the negotiation make a difference? Would Lot and his family have died without Abraham's interference? Was the bargain somehow different because of Abraham's dickering?

If not, what's the point of dealing with God?

BarGaInInG LIKe a CHILD

Psychologist Fritz Oser believes that our modes of bargaining prayer evolve as we physically mature. From his observation of moral development in children, Oser generated a theory that identifies six stages.

Young children begin by seeing the world as guided by an all-powerful Parent, who acts unilaterally and remains for the most part unfazed by appeals. Prayers are not exchanges. Children ask for favors without thought of payments, give without thought of exchange, and receive what comes for what it is.

Around age nine, fair-trading becomes important. As the child's sense of justice grows, prayers take on a bargaining and contractual mode. God can be persuaded—or, if necessary, placated.

But soon (often around age eleven or twelve), children begin to realize that the deals they strike don't always work out as expected. This leads to a faith crisis when they realize they are autonomous creatures with wills of their own. Here they embrace a God they cannot fully understand, or they become Deists or atheists.

When they become adults, those who choose to embrace God enter a fourth level of prayer, "autonomy and salvation," according to Oser. Here they understand God metaphorically through common elements in the world that become symbols of his nature. In the fifth stage, believers recognize that God is love, and they find him in loving relationships, going further in the sixth stage to actively pursuing God by intentionally choosing paths of selflessness.[9]

But Jesus begs to differ with Oser. Instead of encouraging us to "grow up" in our stages of prayer, he beckons us to

35

remain childlike. He says in Matthew's Gospel that, unless we become like little children, we cannot enter the Kingdom of Heaven.[10]

Could it be that this is also true of prayer?

If so, Jesus places toddlers—stage-one children—as role models for those seeking favor with God. Perhaps we progress best when we regress back from the supposed wisdom of maturity to the utter simplicity of childlike giving and receiving. In Oser's scheme, this means moving backward through humanitarianism, universalism, metaphorical idealism, skepticism, and fair-and-square bargaining, to simply asking and receiving.

Jesus tells us what to do.

Ask.

Receive.

He doesn't mention bargaining.

unperstanding the rules

The rules of bartering in God's Kingdom seem to be unlike anything else we have encountered:

- Sometimes we get more than we bargained for.
- Tit for tat is never just that.
- Regardless of how good our deal is, better deals can be made with others and are often flaunted rather than hidden from our view.
- God's generosity appears to be greater than our ability to ask for it.
- Despite his ability to do so, God doesn't force us to pay when we renege on our part of the negotiation. Yet he always keeps his end of the deal.

- We're never clear who it is we're dealing with and whether or not our bargaining has made a difference.

Imagine this type of transaction in the marketplace of a foreign country. We want to bring home a souvenir—perhaps a piece of gold jewelry. We haggle with the seller until we believe we have offered a fair price. In exchange, we get the bracelet.

But in the rules of God's economy, as we take the bracelet back to our hotel and examine it under the light, we notice it is loaded with the finest diamonds. We received a much better deal than we bargained for. What would a seller have to gain by giving us more than we agreed on?

What if the next morning, when we board the tour bus, we learn that the woman across the aisle negotiated a similar bargain with the seller? She got the diamond-encrusted bracelet but also received matching earrings and a necklace. And her diamonds are bigger. Why didn't we get that deal?

What could a seller possibly gain from giving diamonds away to his customers? If a seller did this regularly, we could only assume that *there is more going on*. The price we paid for the bracelet was being exchanged for something else.

But what else could that be?

Many people are uncomfortable with haggling. They don't like the idea of dickering over price. "Just give me a fair price, and I'll pay it," they say. The emergence of new car dealerships with low and nonnegotiable sticker prices seems to confirm this trend. Some of us want to approach God that way. Just tell me the price to pass the test, seal the deal, or get out of the speeding ticket; I'll gladly pay it. Just let me know what it's worth to you.

But like a great negotiator, he asks us to make the first offer.

What are we willing to pay?

We follow with an insultingly low offer. "God, would you supernaturally reverse the course of disease and decay in this world, stop the very natural order of the earth, just this once? If you do, I will put in a few hours at your house on Sunday."

Haggling works with us, so we believe it works with God. This is a big misunderstanding of his character. Maybe he *tolerates* our bargaining because he hopes something greater will occur in the process, just as it did with Abraham. The result of Abraham's negotiation with God was not saving the people of Sodom and Gomorrah. But perhaps Abraham's reward was confirmation that God cared about him, was willing to listen to him, and considered his thoughts.

Could it be that God doesn't bargain for the outcome of the negotiation, but that the process of negotiating is God's way of bargaining with us for something greater?

God isn't in the business of selling chits, onetime favors, or bargains. He is in the business of transforming lives for his own glory. God seems to be saying that the bargains are peripheral and he's happy to engage us in conversation about them, but ultimately, there is only one thing he is willing to trade for—our lives.

No savvy seller sells at a loss.

God won't, either.

To do a straight-up bargain, where we pay our fair share,

is to always leave God with a loss, because the outcome isn't what he is after. We try to win God's favor by bargaining with what we think he wants.

God's answer? He will deal, but only if it's big—everything for everything. "I give all, you give all!" He wants our lives. He is the only one who fully understands what it costs and is willing to pay for it.

God haggles only because we insist on haggling.

He prefers that we just give up the negotiating—that we give it all up and give it to him. If we stop trying to take control of our lives, our situations, and things; if instead we offer them to him, he makes some amazing promises in return. He will take care of all our needs. He will give us eternal life. He will deliver us from evil. He will love us unconditionally.

When we exchange our all for his all, we can then ask and receive. And we will receive exceedingly more than we bargained for.

Martin Luther's Bargain

Martin Luther had a quick wit and a quicker tongue. Throughout his life, he said things he had good reason to later regret. In 1505, Luther had already received a master's degree when, at his father's urging, he enrolled in law school. One day, as he walked near the university, a lightning bolt struck so near him that in panic he cried out, "Help, St. Anne! I'll become a monk!" The storm passed. His life was spared.

Luther regretted his words; yet he kept his promise. Against his father's wishes, he dropped out of law school and entered an Augustinian monastery, where he applied himself fully to the meritorious systems of Medieval Catholicism.

A monk's life encompassed bargain after bargain. Luther, like the pre-Christian Saul of Tarsus, excelled in cutting good-works deals with his Creator. He fasted, repented, served the poor, and vigorously studied both ancient and contemporary scholastic theologians. In 1510, Luther even walked 850 miles to Rome, crawling up the steps of St. Peter's Cathedral to prove he deserved a hearing before God.

But ten years of such rigor moved him no closer to God. His bargains all felt one-sided. The harder he pressed, the deeper the silence. God eluded him. His prayers were not answered.

Then one day in 1514, Luther was locked away in his study, on the second floor of a tower attached to the seminary where he taught. He was reading Paul's letter to the Romans. Suddenly another lightning bolt struck. Though it was only metaphoric, this one didn't miss.

Luther was working his way through the first chapter when he came to the words "righteousness that is by faith." Suddenly his whole world tilted 180 degrees.

Negotiations with God were closed. The deal had been sealed 1,500 years earlier when Jesus had exchanged his perfection for our brokenness. In a flash, Luther realized that his monkish pandering was all nonsense. To bargain with God was to presume the parties held currencies of equal value. The reality, Luther realized, was that we hold nothing of substance.[11]

To offer God compensation for his favors is insulting, like offering to pay the host of an extravagant feast with the change in our pockets. The currency we offer to pay our debts—obedience, good works, faithfulness—is the very stuff of which heaven is made. Like the rich man with the suitcase of gold bricks, we're proudly pouring out pieces of pavement and chunks of concrete. And God is just smiling at the pathetic mess we're making.

We have nothing of worth to offer him. Our currency holds no value in his Kingdom. And even if there were a way for us to exchange our currency for his, he is far too generous to ever be fairly compensated. Instead, all we need to do is accept the gift as given. But in asking to receive that gift, we are in essence exchanging our lives— for his Son's life.

What is the currency of heaven?

Life.

Your life is the only cash God will accept.

What are the rules of commerce?

Ask.

Receive.

Get more than you bargained for.

Are you willing to bargain with God?

Because bargaining prayers are prayers he always answers.

3
STUPID SHAPES, WEIRD COLORS, CROOKED NECKS, AND NO SCREW TOPS
Questioning Prayers

AS DARKNESS FALLS on the outskirts of Garden Ridge, Texas, more than twenty million Mexican freetail bats (equal to the human population of Texas) ascend from the depths of Bracken Cave to hunt for their dinner. Before the night is through, they will devour enough insects to equal the weight of sixty-three elephants. In those first moments after sunset, the sky above Garden Ridge is a screeching mass of chaos.

But it is not what it seems.

Despite the traffic in the skies, there are no bat collisions or even any bat confusion. Every bat in the sky seems to know exactly where it is and where it is going.

Bats are mammals—the only mammals capable of true flight. Though their eyes are of little use once they take to the sky, bats manage to perceive every necessary detail in the world that surrounds them. They use a tool called "echo-location" or sonar. As bats fly, they emit high-pitched sounds at frequencies humans cannot hear. These sounds reflect off surrounding objects and return to the bat's large, sensitive ears. The bat's brain then decodes the sounds, filtering out the clutter, to give the bat a precise picture of the location and size of all objects around it. By sending sounds out into the invisible world and waiting to hear what comes back, the bat is able to make sense of its own place in the world.

As humans, we do the same thing, except we use questions instead of echolocation:

> Who's there?
> Do you love me?
> What's my purpose?

We use questions as our spiritual sonar. The answers that come back reveal whether we're alone, loved, or have a purpose in life. The response, or lack of response, that comes back provides information about our place in the world. Nowhere is this truer than when we try to prove the existence of God. We send out questions and can only wait to see if he responds.

Are we alone?

Paul Allen, cofounder of Microsoft, leads a team of high-tech tycoons, including Intel's Gordon Moore and Cisco Systems' Sandy Lerner, in funding the Search for Extraterrestrial Intelligence Institute (SETI). With a healthy share of Allen's personal fortune (estimated at $20 billion), the institute is building 350 radio telescopes on the north coast of

California, aiming them into the expanse of space in hopes of finding a sign that humans are not alone in the cosmos.[1]

And why not? It's a big universe, and it's getting bigger every millisecond. With hundreds of billions of stars in our galaxy and hundreds of billions of galaxies beyond, there must be numerous warm pools of muck out there where life can accidentally begin and start the slow march toward becoming creatures that make cell phones and ballistic missiles.

SETI's plan seems reasonable. Radio telescopes systematically scan millions of neighborhood star systems, analyzing emitted signals for "nonrandom" patterns that might transmit communications. Such patterns, SETI scientists contend, would certainly imply design, and design would imply intelligence and intent. Their project is slated to take twenty-five years and millions of dollars to complete. The adventure is exhilarating. "The sheer knowledge that another civilization exists—that would be an amazing thing," says Allen.[2]

Allen and his team are not consciously seeking contact with a transcendent spirit. But by training their satellite dishes on distant star systems and asking, "Hey, is anyone up there?" they are, in another sense, asking, "Hey, is anyone *way* up there?"

The field of science is ripe for such questions.

A Scientist's Wager

Blaise Pascal was thirty-one years old in 1654. By that time, he had already revolutionized the construction of mechanical calculators, the study of fluids, the concepts of pressure and vacuum, projective geometry, probability theory (which provided the groundwork for today's study of economics and social science), and the scientific method itself.

Evidently, conquering the known world wasn't enough. Pascal had deeper questions, about the deepest matters. What stood behind this wondrous, orderly world he was discovering? Was there really a God out there? He longed to be certain.

Pascal knew by heart the traditional arguments for God's existence. Medieval philosophers had reasoned these out centuries before, but as a child of the Enlightenment, Pascal also knew a rebuttal or two for each of these points. If reason was the measure, proving God was proving impossible.

Until November 23, 1654—the day Pascal "met" God.

Though he communicated little of this encounter, he wrote of it and sewed the sheets of paper inside the lining of his coat. The moment changed the course of his life. He dropped his scientific studies and set out to build a bridge between his spiritual experience and the discipline of logical argument. His great unfinished work, *Pensées*, recounts his amazing quest.

Unable to confirm God's existence and unwilling to discount the validity of his own connection with God, Pascal split the difference. True to his inventive, pragmatic nature, he devised a probability case for why believing in God made more sense than not believing. We call it "Pascal's Wager." It runs roughly like this:

> If I believe in God and I'm right, I gain everything for all eternity.
> If I believe in God and I'm wrong, there is no God and death is my absolute end. I lose nothing by believing

in Him, but gain inner peace and love for and from
my fellow man.

If, however, I disbelieve in God and I'm right, I gain
nothing, for death is my absolute end.

And of course, if I disbelieve in God and I'm wrong,
I lose everything for all eternity.[3]

So, "God, are you there?"

Pascal's hot tip: The smart money bets *yes*.

Why?

"The heart has reasons that reason cannot know," wrote
Pascal, suggesting that this scientist saw the need for something greater than logical reasoning.

unbalanced

Scientists aren't the only ones who ask questions about
the existence of God. In the 1970s, author Judy Blume published a book called *Are You There God? It's Me, Margaret*.
Decades later, the book is still popular. Ostensibly, the story
is about a girl struggling to come to terms with changes
taking place inside her body and mind as she approaches
adolescence. But equally confusing to her is her relationship with God.

It's interesting how often confusion from one area of our
lives bubbles over into another.

The words "Are you there, God?" arise from different
souls, in different moments, in wildly diverse situations. But
as humans, we consistently use these words not to demand
proof of his existence but to look for his presence to fulfill a
common, yet vague yearning.

We want to know whether or not we are alone.

Like a preprogrammed chip in an electronic toy, could it be that we are somehow born with the question embedded in us?

Perhaps it simply awaits the right moment to float to the surface, like a bubble of air in a bottle submerged under the sea. That air pocket sits at rest until some change of tide tilts the bottle and disturbs the equilibrium. Maybe the prayer "God, are you there?" is what escapes us whenever *we* become unbalanced.

Ten-year-old Matthew fell out of balance in Juarez, Mexico. A typical American boy with boundless energy, a mess of dark hair, and a lopsided grin, Matthew was trained in age-appropriate theology at his church, tutored in faith by his homeschooling mother, and lived in a church community that confirmed his worldview. He believed with all his heart that God existed and that God was good. But the faith rope on which he swung frayed the day that new evidence unsettled his beliefs—beliefs he thought had long been resolved.

Following the free-trade agreements between the United States and Mexico, Juarez became a haven for millions of Mexican villagers seeking employment. Divided from El Paso, Texas, by a barbed-wire wall and the Rio Grande River, Juarez turned into a cesspool of corruption due to rapid growth and an expanding drug trade. In the stampede for survival, the indigent became surplus baggage.

Twenty miles outside of Juarez stands a compound about half the size of a city block. The gates are still under construction, but they open into a wide courtyard lined with small rooms. The place is filled with people—troubled, ailing, and smelly people.

Approximately eighty men and women live inside these plastered walls, all having been rescued from the barrios of Juarez, where they had been left for dead. Many are physically handicapped. Most suffer from mental illness. Some have minds and bodies ravaged from habitually sniffing glue.

As Matthew and his dad toured the compound, they saw men and women held in cages for their own—and others'—protection. They were screaming like rabid cats while curled up in their own waste. This was how they spent every waking hour. They were barely recognizable as human.

Dad watched the tears pool in his brave son's brown eyes.

The experience confused and horrified Matthew. He had been taught that God was good. That he loved everyone. That he was ever-present. And that Jesus saves.

But as Matthew looked around this place full of needy people, he didn't see God, and he didn't see anything good. The scene before him suggested that everything he knew about God was wrong. If God loves and saves, why didn't he love and save these people?

Matthew was asking if God existed. He couldn't articulate his question out loud, but his father read it in his eyes. *God, if you're really out there, why aren't you here?*

We ask questions.

Is there anyone out there?

Does anyone care about me?

Do I have a purpose that's greater than what I see?

Is there a God?

These are also the questions that we pray.

49

FOrMING THE *ReaL* QueSTION
Is there a God?

A philosophy professor asked only one question on the final exam. He picked up a chair, put it on his desk, and wrote on the board, "Using everything we have learned this semester, prove that this chair does not exist." The class dug deep and wrote passionately for the whole hour—some churning out thirty pages of heady philosophical debate and logic.

In less than a minute, one student folded his paper, stood, and turned it in. He was the only student to get an A. What wisdom and knowledge did he use to prove the chair didn't exist? He simply wrote, "What chair?"

Is there a God?

Answering that question in the affirmative requires proof of *existence*. Humans have sought proof of the gods since the beginning of recorded history. But the unqualified answer has always eluded us. And unless some genie-god appears in a cloud of smoke and lets us take him on a sort of adult show-and-tell to all doubters, it's unlikely we'll ever have irrefutable proof. Believers of any faith can prattle on with anecdotal arguments full of coincidences that to them prove the presence of God. But assertion doesn't prove existence.

It never will.

And maybe that's how God wants it.

Perhaps he even made us in such a way that there could never be enough proof of his existence.

Christians believe the Bible is the inspired Word of God. It seems that if God wanted to prove his existence, he could do it within those pages. "Snap your fingers and I will appear. Test me on this right now. If I don't appear, I don't exist." You won't find any such invitation in the Bible. God chooses not to prove his existence.

In fact, the Gospels often speak about people who came in contact with Jesus—the very Son of God. They saw his miracles, heard his wise words, and yet refused to believe in him. Even his own followers occasionally had trouble believing and asked for proof, the most famous doubter being the apostle Thomas.

Theologically, we may be dancing around the issue of free will, but could there be more to it?

Proving beyond a reasonable doubt that God exists might pacify our curiosity, but it still wouldn't satisfy our deepest yearning—to fulfill our loneliness.

So what if we changed the question?

Rather than ask, "Is there a God?" maybe we should ask, "Is anyone there?" or even, "God, are you there?"

There's a difference.

The question, "God, are you there?" is not an appeal for a change in circumstances; it is a quest for assurance.

The right response is not an action, but an *insight*.

The new question requires proof of *experience*. To satisfactorily answer it, we don't need the kind of proofs that stand up to academic and scientific rigor; we need the kind of proofs that reassure our senses. We can answer this question affirmatively only when we hear, touch, taste, see, or smell God. With this question, we are no longer asking God for proof of his *existence*, but rather for proof of his *presence*.

Our minds want facts, but could it be that our emotions and imaginations would settle for *less* proof in order to secure *more* experience? Could this need for experiencing God be satisfied with his presence through what the Bible calls "the touch of his hand" and "the sound of his voice"?

RISKY QUESTIONS

Of course, this new question is far more dangerous. We consider the existence question out of intellectual curiosity or boredom. But the presence question raises the stakes.

We ask, but do we really want the answer?

You return home to an empty house after a long trip. You flip on a light, set your keys on the counter, and glance through the mail. Distracted, you think you hear a sound upstairs. Slowly you set down the bills. You hear it again. Nerve endings tingle in the back of your throat as you try to swallow. Your senses heighten. You can hear your heartbeat. Thoughts of fight or flight enter and leave your mind. Every muscle tenses as you recognize that *someone is in the house.*

"Who's there?" you ask . . . but you'd rather not know.

Each of us asks questions, but we're not always sure we want the answers.

Are you going to give me a ticket?

Do you still love me?

Am I going to lose my job?

Where were you last night?

Is she breathing?

God, are you there?

For questions like these, we may not want an answer—unless it's the answer we want. Like Paul Allen and the folks at SETI, like Matthew in Mexico, like the fear of a stranger in our house, we don't know what will change until after we ask the question, and the answers have the potential to change our lives in dramatic, unalterable ways.

God, are you out there?

Does anybody care about me?

Can you give me a sign?

As a young girl, Jennifer attended a Catholic school. Her family traditions, faith community, and education were deeply rooted in the mysteries of the church, so it's not surprising that some of those wonders spilled into her social time as well.

Jennifer recalls a late-night slumber party where the girls played a game of truth or dare. Jennifer's dare involved going into a dark room, staring into the mirror, and saying "Bloody Mary" three times. Though the game's origins are probably associated with tales of a reputed witch named Mary Worth, who appeared in mirrors when beckoned, to a young Catholic girl the phrase "bloody Mary" had an entirely different meaning. Jennifer wouldn't take the dare because she feared what her friends had said would happen if she did—the bloody image of Mary, the mother of Jesus, would appear in the mirror.

A smart girl, Jennifer knew it wasn't likely to happen, but the mysticism and mysteries of the Catholic Church included a rich tradition of statues that wept tears of blood, rosaries that turned to gold when dipped in a fountain, and miraculous healings in foreign places like Lourdes and Fatima.

Jennifer remembered when she was first frightened by the idea of a divine appearance. Watching movies like *The Song of Bernadette* made the possibility of divine appearances real. This film tells the story of a peasant girl who claimed to see a beautiful woman at the city dump in Lourdes, France. Miracles took place in the healing waters of the grotto, and the town was transformed by these events. In another film, *The Miracle of Our Lady of Fatima*, three shepherd children have visions of a lovely lady in a cloud. Despite adult opposition, the children stick to their story. Based on the actual events of the summer of 1917 in Fatima, Portugal, the movie ends when a thousand spectators witness a miracle in the lady's final appearance.

Is God out there?

Could he be here?

Jennifer didn't really want to know.

She remembered having to retrieve items from her parents' master bathroom, located in a dark, interior basement room of her childhood home. On the long countertop nearest the doorway stood a statue of the Virgin Mary, dressed in blue robes with outstretched arms, a golden halo around her head. Standing in the doorway to the bathroom, Jennifer could see the back of the statue reflected in the mirror, giving Mary an unusually lifelike dimension. Every time Jennifer went into that bathroom, she feared the statue would come alive.

Did the statue's eyes move?

Is Mary watching?

What does she want from me?

At the slumber party, Jennifer chose "truth" in the truth or dare game. She refused to stand in front of the mirror and call for "Bloody Mary," because she believed it was possible for the Virgin Mary to appear. In fact, she lived in fear of it.

Jennifer wasn't just afraid of a supernatural appearance;

she was also afraid that her life would change in ways she didn't want it to change.

How would we respond if we were absolutely convinced that God is out there?

Or *right here*?

Imagine asking if God were real, and then like a genie from a bottle, he magically appeared before us. Would we want that?

Would he ask for something?

How would our lives change?

Would we be willing to make those changes?

Are we willing to risk life as we know it, by asking not only if God exists, but if he is present?

Sometimes we're willing to take the risk. When our equilibrium is tilted, the questioning prayer bubbles up. Then, like a bat with sonar sending signals into the unknown and listening for the response, we use the echoes that return to help us understand who we are, what obstacles are ahead of us, and our size and position in the world. Answers can provide confirmation to the hope we seek. Or forever extinguish it. Either way, we put our hope at stake when we simply have to know, *Is anyone there?*

UNEXPECTED ECHOES

Elijah the prophet was one who would go to any extreme. He once walked forty days into the desert and climbed a mountain to find God. The experience nearly cost him his life. Elijah was already at a point of deep depression, crippled by physical and emotional exhaustion. He had recently experienced great victories for God's cause. But on the downside he fell into the grip of despair and even prayed for God to take his life. Elijah hit bottom. That was when he decided to climb.[4]

He set out for a logical place: Horeb, the mountain where Moses had met God and received the Ten Commandments. If Elijah needed to find God, he'd be wise to go where God had shown himself in the past.

"God, are you up there? I'll climb up to find out!"

The trip took weeks. When Elijah arrived at Horeb, he scaled the summit, found a cave for shelter, and waited for God to show up.

But Elijah would be disappointed.

On the mountaintop, he braced himself for an encounter. It came. There were great flashes of fire. An earthquake shook the mountainside. A violent wind tore boulders loose and sent them tumbling.

Signs.

"God, are you there?" Elijah screamed into the raging elements.

Nothing. The signs were merely signs. They were not God.

God, the story says, was not in the fire or the quake or the wind. God was not where Elijah had expected him to be.

Then, as the storms died away, Elijah covered his head and walked to the mouth of the cave. From that vista, he peered out at the world below him. "God, are you out there?"

This time, the answer came. Instead of turbulence and terror, God's voice to Elijah was "still and small." God whispered, "Why are you here?"

Then, instead of praising Elijah's valor and sacrifice, the voice sent him home. "Go back down the mountain and finish the work I gave you."

That was it?

That was it.

Sometimes the answer we get isn't the one we've sought.

Looking for Hidden Treasure

Mark and his buddies were nine years old and in search of buried treasure. On the edge of an old farm field, they found a dump, and for days they dug and uncovered junk, certain that one day they'd stumble upon a treasure chest. And Mark knew what that box would contain. It would contain gold. Just like in the movies.

Instead, all they found were some old glass bottles, with "stupid shapes, weird colors, crooked necks, and no screw tops." Between efforts to get at the treasure that was surely buried below, they hurled the bottles against a huge rock that clung to the side of the hill. This continued for days.

As boys will do, Mark brought a piece of the broken glass home to his mother. A quick inspection and a few questions from Mom revealed that Mark and his friends had shattered a couple thousand dollars worth of antique glass. The treasure he'd found wasn't the treasure he'd been looking for.

Finding God-treasure is the grand ambition of humankind. We have an internal impulse to shed the mantle of flesh, climb a great mountain of self-denial, and enter into a transcendental realm. We want to touch God, see him, be one with him in his world. History is the story of humanity trying to make this climb to God. The resulting strategies are called religion (or possibly science). Each is a theory of how to get through to where God is—an attempt to be spiritual.

The problem is that our experiences almost always fall

short. Aren't our lives marked much more often by the confusing, troubling awareness that we are not one with God?
that we are separated and utterly distinct from him? The
fact that we ask, "God, are you there?" seems to say that
while we long to be "one" with him, we clearly are not. In
fact, we are wholly other.

Moreover, it seems as if God intends it to be this way. He
appears to resist overshadowing us with his power. One of
the ancient Hebrew names for God is *Yahweh Shammah*,
"the God who is there." God is *there*. But *there* means outside, separate—even hiding, perhaps, just enough to make
things interesting and to ensure that we can know and be
known.

Does God hide?

It's possible.

After all, if we were not separate from God, how could
we come to love him, and how could he come to love us?

But maybe God's elusive nature and our unquenchable
yearning for him are themselves the biggest proof of his
presence. Genesis says that when God created, he separated. He moved things apart, first from himself, then from
other things. Creation meant severing ties.

Even Jesus felt the loneliness of separation. The apostle
Paul says that when Jesus was born he had to empty
himself of all the benefits of his divine nature.[5] How lonely
that must have been. But it got worse. Matthew tells us
that when they nailed Jesus to the cross, he cried out,
quoting Psalm 22, "My God, my God, why have you forsaken me?"[6]

Christians believe that, at that moment, the effects of all
the sin and sorrow of time came crashing down on his body

and he bore it. When that happened, even God, his Father, could not bear to look upon him. God turned away, and Jesus felt the full desperation of sudden, complete separation from him.

Loneliness is a universal human experience.

And Jesus was fully human.

So God flipped the tables. Instead of telling us how to get spiritual, God became material. He came to be with us, to be found right here and now. Down to earth. That is essentially the story of Christianity—God come to earth. We don't have to find him; he has found us.

We instinctively know he is here—there—somewhere, which is why we are compelled to seek him. So, we climb a mountain—or better yet, like our ancestors at Babel, we build one of our own. We go high. After all, mountains are the natural place to ask the big questions. And while we're up there, we feel in control. The high ground gives us battle advantage.

What do we find in these mountaintop experiences?

The same thing Elijah found.

Perhaps a rare, momentary epiphany, some quick sliver of revelation. But those transcendent insights never last. Monday's reality sets in. The wonder lifts, and we're sent back down the mountain into a vague disappointment.

We ask until we see that God is not in the fire or the wind or the earthquake. Then we sit still and wait for answers. God was not in the wind, the fire, or the earthquake for Elijah, but for Moses he was a burning bush, and for Paul he was in his blindness. Could it be that we're sometimes blind to where he is?

Could it be that it isn't the answers, the facts, or the

proofs that we (and Elijah) need—could it be we need the experience?

The fact that *we ask* is proof that *God exists*.

What we seek is the experience of God.

If we ask, he will answer—with his presence.

MAXIMIZING THE EXPERIENCE

The late novelist Ayn Rand, an acknowledged atheist, was speaking before an audience at Yale University when a reporter asked this question: "What's wrong with the modern world?"

Her reply was insightful: "Never before has the world been so desperately asking for answers to crucial questions, and never before has the world been so frantically committed to the idea that no answers are possible. To paraphrase the Bible, the modern attitude is, Father forgive us, for we know not what we are doing—and please don't tell us!"[7]

Rand understood that we want the experience, but we don't want to be changed by the experience.

Talking to God is serious business. Once we enter a conversation—one he's baited us into—we may end up with more than we bargained for. He's flirting with us, teasing us to flirt back. When we open the door with "Are you there?" he responds by stepping up his pursuit of us.

It's a game that can quickly get out of hand. Coming on to God can get us into trouble. He takes the words "Are you there?" with passionate seriousness. Even when we think we're toying with philosophy, he's playing for keeps, and he may snatch up the chance to make a move. It's courtship, and God is a master romantic.

Remember Matthew, the boy whose faith was shaken

when he visited hell in Mexico? Matthew didn't see the "God is good" of his childhood prayers. His faith trembled. Where is God, if he's not here?

But God was there. Matthew just didn't see him. Like Elijah, who was looking for God in earthquakes and hurricanes and floods, but he found him in a still, small voice. Like Mark and the boys tossing unrecognized treasures against a rock. Like all of us asking, "Is there a God?" instead of "God, are you there?"

Matthew's answer was in the question itself. And his father recognized it. Grabbing his son by the hand, he dragged him to meet a man named José Antonio.

José Antonio Galván had tried and failed twice as a pastor in America. But while visiting Juarez, he asked God for a third chance. While wandering the streets of the city, he found himself staring into the vacant eyes of the homeless. "God, what can I do?" he cried out.

The answer came as a shocking idea, a proposal of sorts that filled and then abducted José Antonio's imagination. If he wanted a church, there were plenty of members here. All he needed to do was gather them off the streets. So José Antonio raised money. Then he built the remarkable compound, Visión en Acción, and filled it with those who needed it most—the sick and the poor that he found on the streets of Juarez.

Since then, his idea has fostered some remarkable transformations. Like Hector, who lived a life on the streets that was worse than death. José Antonio and his team brought Hector home to the compound, where they fed him, read him Bible stories, and by the power of the Holy Spirit chased off his demons.

Twelve months later, Hector, with his toothless grin, followed Pastor Galván around the sanctuary like a dancing puppy. Happy, fed, and smiling, but still incomplete, he was evidence that God was working through José Antonio's question, "What can I do?"

That was the missing link for Matthew. God hadn't forsaken these people; other people had.

"God, are you there?"

For Matthew, the question wasn't answered with a hurricane of healing, an earthquake of aid, or a flood of relief; it was answered by experiencing God through José Antonio and Hector. It was experienced by asking himself the question that God wants all of us to ask as a result of being in his presence: "God, what can I do?" "God, are you there?"

The answer comes because he has already come himself.

The answer comes when he proposes and we accept.

The answer comes when we share our vows and consummate our covenant by consenting to be transformed by the experience.

God always answers bargaining prayers. He also answers questioning prayers—even when the questions are about him.

We may use our spiritual sonar to ask where we are in relation to things greater than ourselves. But what do we do with the experience we receive as a result of these questions?

Perhaps we can be more like the bats of Garden Ridge, Texas, and allow the echoing signals to guide our sense of place and purpose.

4
THE PRAYER GOD RARELY ANSWERS

SHORTLY BEFORE JENNIFER'S EIGHTH BIRTHDAY, her family knew something was wrong. It started with occasional complaints of headaches during her third-grade reading class. But her mother, Marie, also began to notice other unusual behaviors. Jennifer started getting out of bed frequently—ostensibly to use the bathroom. Pregnant with her seventh child, Marie valued those rare moments when the kids were tucked in bed; it was the only time during the day when she and her husband, Paul, could have a private conversation. Though Jennifer had been a compliant child, Marie began to suspect ulterior motives. Was Jennifer getting up so she could listen in on those conversations?

There were other clues that something wasn't right. Though Jennifer was thin, maybe even a little too skinny, she ate an incredible amount of food. Marie often caught her ravaging through the cupboards, eating whatever she could find and yet complaining there wasn't enough food.

One Friday afternoon in October, Jennifer came home from school and ate seven peanut butter and jelly sandwiches. Later, the family went out to dinner. At the restaurant, Jennifer didn't order anything to eat, but the waitress couldn't keep her glass filled. As Marie watched her daughter drain glass after glass of liquid, she realized that even pregnant, she couldn't drink or eat as much as her eight-year-old daughter. Marie left Jennifer with her grandmother for the weekend and went home to review her medical books from nursing school. Something was definitely wrong.

When Jennifer returned home on Sunday, her energy was gone. She sat, and then lay, on the couch. Everything seemed fuzzy. She stared at the ceiling.

Her grandmother reported taking Jennifer to a movie earlier that afternoon and buying, at Jennifer's request, an extra-large Coke. When Jennifer asked for a refill, her grandmother had refused. Driven by an insatiable thirst, Jennifer asked if she could refill it at the water fountain. She did—twice. Between trips to the bathroom and refilling the cup, Jennifer missed most of the movie.

Her unusual behavior justified Marie's suspicions.

On Monday morning, Marie took Jennifer to the doctor, where her fears were confirmed. Normal blood sugar levels range from 60 to 120. Jennifer's was 830—juvenile diabetes. In the mid-1970s, a diagnosis of diabetes wasn't a death sentence, but it was a life sentence. Treatment was available, but it meant big lifestyle changes. The whole family had to accommodate Jennifer's new diet and strict schedule for eating and taking insulin. Though Marie and Paul grieved the diagnosis—they wished it had been one of them rather than their daughter—Jennifer seemed to adjust to her new life.

Months later, Marie was talking on the phone to her sister and remarking how well everyone had adapted. "She's never even asked why she got it or why her. She's had a great attitude about the whole thing."

Jennifer overheard the conversation. A few days later when she didn't get her way about something insignificant, she retreated to her room in a pout and started writing in her diary, "Why me?" "Why did I have to get diabetes?" "Why did this happen?"

In Jennifer's case, *why* wasn't a concern until she overheard her mother say that it was.

Whereas bargaining prayers are provoked by circumstances, questioning prayers bubble to the surface and erupt.

They happen instinctively.

So where does *why* come from?

Does it erupt forcefully from within?

Does it gush uncontrollably?

Could it be that *why* prayers aren't an instinctual response, but a learned one?

DON'T ASK WHY!

Why me?

Why did I lose my job?

Why did he have to die?

Why didn't the chemo work?

Why didn't you answer my prayer?

Why can't I?

Why didn't you?

God is a big target for our big questions. Though *why* may be the easiest prayer to utter, it is often the most troublesome. And it's one that God seldom seems to answer.

Why is that?

Why is primeval, a perennial root word that has survived all the bitter winters that have tested the human genome. We start blabbering "Why?" as soon as we can talk.

"Why is the sky blue?"

"Why can't my ears swallow peas?"

"Why can't I pinch the baby?"

"Why can't I use crayons on the wall?"

Though inquisitive three-year-olds may exasperate their mothers with *Why? Why? Why?* by the time these kids reach elementary school, they will have learned to leverage the question to their advantage.

"It's time for bed!"

"Why do I have to go to bed?"

"Because it is 9:15 and you have school tomorrow."

"Why do I have to go to bed now?"

"Because we want you to do well in school, and you can't if you're tired."

"Why do I have to go to school?"

"Because you need a good education to succeed in the world."

"Why do I have to succeed?"

"Because . . . because I said so! Get to bed!"

Teenagers often use *why* questions to plead their case: *"Everybody else is going; why can't I?"*

After eighteen years of learning how to answer the question, parents of teenagers skip to the only answer that puts the question on simmer until the next outburst: "Because I said so!"

That's often how we think of God, isn't it?

We ask *why* and we don't get a response. We picture God up in his heavenly office, looking like George Burns, cigar dangling out of his mouth, feet propped on the desk playing Sinatra's "I Did It My Way" in the background as he stamps, "Because I Said So" on all the *why* prayer requests that pass through his in-box.

God the Father . . .

of us . . .

his insolent teenagers.

Does God get irritated?

Clearly, he does. The Bible shows us occasions where God's ire is raised, but never by sincere questions. And *why* is often the sincerest of questions.

We really want to know.

Or do we?

THE LONG ANSWER

The problem with *why* is that it is often a bottomless pit of a question. Given an answer to a precise question, *why* trumps every retort, because *why* can never be fully satisfied. The question *why* gives the inquisitor the last word, if not the final say. As a presumptuous quest to know a cause, *why* is futile. Yes, God knows the final answer to the final question, but he remains hard-pressed to put such a complicated answer into words that make sense to us.

After all, some questions are more complicated than others. When we see an elderly friend at the grocery store, we offer a polite greeting, "How are you?"

We don't really want her to recount her prescription list or the stories behind each ailment they aim to cure. Nor do we want to probe her inner psyche. We just want to buy our milk and bread and go home.

"How are you?" is an infinitely complicated question.

When we're asked, the merciful response would be, "Do you want the short answer or the truth?"

But politeness prevents the questioner from saying, "Neither."

Some questions get us in too deep, dredging up bottom filth we never bargained for.

Some questions are just too big.

Why is one of them.

In the film *A Few Good Men*, Jack Nicholson plays a military commander who must testify in a court martial for U.S. Marines on trial for murder. When Tom Cruise, the lawyer prosecuting the case, puts Nicholson on the witness stand and demands the truth, Nicholson snarls, "You can't handle the truth!" Things are much more complex than we imagine and far more interwoven than we can understand. Perhaps we can't handle the truth of *why*.

When we ask God *why*, we are asking him to pluck out one cause and explain it without consideration as to what came before and what follows after. All he can do is reply truthfully, "Do you want the long or short answer?" Perhaps we don't want either one.

In 1961, meteorologist Edward Lorenz was trying to predict weather patterns using a numerical model. While retesting his results, he rounded his initial value to three digits, rather than entering the full six-digit number that the computer could calculate. The result was a

markedly different outcome. Applying the principles of
chaos theory, Lorenz noted that small changes in initial
conditions can result in wildly different results. He published his findings.

Several years later, Lorenz was scheduled to give a talk
on the topic of "sensitive dependence" at a meeting of the
American Association for the Advancement of Science.
When the time came to submit the program title, fellow
meteorologist Philip Merilees, who was set to convene the
meeting, was unable to confirm Lorenz's title with him. So,
instead, he posed the question, *Does the flap of a butterfly's
wings in Brazil set off a tornado in Texas* as the title.
Thus, the term *butterfly effect* was coined to describe intri-
cately connected cause and effect.[1]

The butterfly effect gives some insight into how long a
long answer can be.

In an episode of *The Simpsons*, a less sophisticated
illustration of the same principle features Homer traveling
back in time. The trivial swat of a mosquito results in his
neighbor Ned Flanders's ruling the world. And when Homer
sneezes, he wipes out the dinosaurs, resulting in wealth,
well-behaved kids, dead sisters-in-law, and donuts raining
from the sky.[2]

Imagine asking God, "Why is it raining donuts?"

Perhaps more understandable is Frank Capra's delightful post-World War II film, *It's a Wonderful Life*. George
Bailey, suicidal and despondent, is shown by an angel how
the world would have been tragically different had he never
been born.

These popular cultural examples illustrate a truth we
already know—each action from each living soul has a

butterfly effect on the world. In short, *why* is too complicated; we can't handle the truth.

To get an honest answer from God, to have him actually
sort out causes from effects and tell us the details, would
require an answer so incomprehensible it would take six
billion years to download, and perhaps even longer to
decipher.

The long answer is . . .

Well . . .

Do you have long enough to sit and listen to the full
story?

Is there a short answer?

There might be.

We may have even been given the short answer, but as
with a child, a short and simple answer to *why* usually
results in more *why* questions. *Why* isn't an essay question
to be answered in one hundred words or less.

where's the fairness?

"If I told you why, would it change anything?"

This was the challenge posed to Job.

Poor, suffering Job. In the opening stanzas of the Old
Testament poem that bears his name, Job has a good life. He
is wealthy, influential, and has good kids. But his fortunes
take a sudden, unexpected, and—in his mind—unfair turn
when God, *his God*, turns him over to suffer abuse at the
hands of Satan. Job becomes the ante in a kind of cosmic
poker match.

Satan contends to God that Job is faithful only because
he receives favor.

"Remove that favor," Satan says, "and Job will curse you!"

God takes the challenge and allows Satan to wreak havoc on Job's life.

Job's family is decimated, his wealth consumed, and his health destroyed. He's ruined. After the dust settles on the compounded disasters, Job, dressed in sackcloth, sits and weeps on a pile of ashes.

His grief is crushing. His confusion debilitating.

To Job, this turn of events seems wildly unjust. He passionately believes he is innocent of anything that justifies such punishment. Job's experience of undeserved suffering leads him straight to the top. "I want to see the manager—of the universe."

When God doesn't appear, Job does the only thing he can reasonably imagine: He sues God—*in absentia*.

Job instigates litigation, calling God as both defendant and judge to look at the evidence and verify Job's innocence. The bulk of the long poem depicts Job fielding challenging questions from three friends, who join the trial as voluntary "defenders" of God's case.

"Surely," his friends argue, "you have done something to warrant this disaster. God is always fair. Bad things befall bad people. Good things come to good people. There must be a sin somewhere." Job adamantly rejects each charge and repeatedly affirms his innocence.

The friends' arguments are technically sound. Sound but empty. That's the basis of Job's metaphorical lawsuit—his confusion over the fairness of his friends' arguments. It is true that God has bound himself to keep certain promises. If God is fair, he should reward good and punish evil. Job believes he has honored his side of the bargain, and he petitions God to keep his. The law on which the merits are argued is God's law and God's promises, with God's character as an *a priori* assumption. In essence, Job is holding God's feet to the fire of his own holy Word.

Heaven's courts are jammed at this very hour with litigants filing grievances against God.

> "I led the Boy Scout troop, and my son got into drugs."
> "I gave money to the poor, and my business went under."
> "I ate right and exercised and had a heart attack."

Where, then, is the fairness?

Silence.

And so it is with Job. Throughout the book, back and forth from challenge to counter-challenge, defense to counter-defense, God stands silent. He makes no response to the subpoena, nor will he even testify on his own behalf. Thirty-seven of Job's forty chapters are Godless.

BE CAREFUL WHAT YOU ASK FOR

Jesus fielded questions the way Ozzie Smith fielded grounders at shortstop—with fluid, effortless panache. Instead of answering directly, he almost always volleyed the question back to the inquisitor. Jesus loved to turn tables—literally and figuratively.

John's Gospel is filled with people peppering Jesus with questions. Some are urgent, passion driven, personal.

"Why has this happened?"

Others are impersonal, abstract, theological.

"How does the universe work?"

Either way, people seldom got what they expected when they interrogated Jesus.

Nicodemus, a leading member of the Jewish religious establishment, tried to play it safe, but his caution got him in over his head. Nicodemus had a reputation and position to protect, so he arranged a secret, after-hours interview with Jesus. Like many of his contemporaries, he'd heard about Jesus and was curious to know more.

"We know you are a teacher sent from God . . . ," he began. But he never got to his real question. What he really intended to ask was, "Are you the Messiah?" Most Jews who heard Jesus teach or witnessed his miracles wondered this.

But Jesus cut to the chase. "Your own identity, not mine, is the first question at hand," Jesus said. "You imagine that because of family lineage you have special privilege from God. Being born a Jew is not a ticket to heaven, Nicodemus; you must be *born again*."

By this, Jesus meant that something miraculous had to be "conceived" in Nicodemus. He needed a new identity, a change at the very deepest level of his nature—something he could never accomplish himself.

This wasn't exactly what Nicodemus expected when he asked the question.[3]

In the very next chapter of John, we see Jesus sitting beside a well in the region of Samaria. His students have gone into the village of Sychar to secure lunch. While Jesus waits, a woman approaches. It's noon and it's hot.

Most women came to the well early in the morning. They traveled in groups, talked about their husbands and kids, and the work somehow seemed lighter. But this woman came alone. Jesus starts a conversation with her by asking her for a drink. This in itself was remarkable. Jewish rabbis never spoke directly to women. And to address a Samaritan, whom the Jews believed were racially and religiously inferior, was apostasy. But Jesus never knelt at the altar of convention.

He asks her for water.

Then he promises her "living water."

She is perplexed by this. She ponders it and then decides to take him up on his offer, "So I won't get thirsty and have to keep coming here."

But as in his conversation with Nicodemus, Jesus flips the tables on her expectations. "Go, call your husband," he says.

"I don't have a husband."

Jesus replies, "You're right. You've had five husbands, and the man you're living with now is not your husband." He knows things about her.

Exposed, the woman runs for cover by changing the subject. "So," she asks, "since you are obviously a prophet and know such things, where is the right place to worship? What, pray tell, is the true religion?" Anything to keep Jesus from hounding her soul.

"None of that matters," he replies. "True worshipers worship anywhere. How about you?"

Though preachers and teachers have pulled countless messages from these brief stories, perhaps the obvious warning is to be careful what you ask. Jesus is a dangerous conversationalist. He can turn even the most casual encounter into an open-heart conversation.

WHY BACK AT YOU

After thirty-seven chapters of silence, at the very moment when Job's frustration nearly crosses the border into blasphemy, God finally speaks.

He appears and answers the charge.

Almost.

Instead of responding to Job's "why?" or ruling on Job's innocence, God flips the tables. Instead of answering Job's questions, he asks a few of his own.

"Where were you when I made the heavens?"

Yikes!

"Where were you when I made elephants and stars and whales and quarks?

"Job, how experienced are you? How smart are you? How old are you? You are demanding to know *why*. Do you have ten billion years for me to explain all the intricacies and contingencies of my universe and how your petty experiences in this vast cosmos really do affirm my justice and love? Because they do.

"Do you have time to listen to *why*?

"Do you have enough understanding to fathom the truth, even if I were to explain it? Can you bear the truth, the whole truth, and nothing but the truth, so help you me?

"Do you have the brainpower?

"If you do, then you and I would be equal. But you are not my equal. So, little man, do you want the long answer or the short answer? The long answer would explode your mind into nothingness. And the short answer . . . the short answer is simple: I AM. Shall we simply leave it at that?"

Job does. He drops his head in his hands and drops his charges. And with those drops, he affirms that God is God.

In *The Message*, Eugene Peterson eloquently expresses Job's response: "I admit it. I was the one. I babbled on about things far beyond me, made small talk about wonders way over my head."[4]

Understand what is happening here:

Job isn't satisfied with easy answers. His friends tried that, and Job wouldn't let it rest.

God wasn't asking Job to forget his question.

He wasn't telling Job not to ask.

He gave Job an answer that was as incomprehensible as God is. Only when the answer got too big for Job was Job satisfied that his question was too small.

"I admit I once lived by rumors of you; now I have it all firsthand—from my own eyes and ears! I'm sorry—forgive me. I'll never do that again, I promise! I'll never again live on crusts of hearsay, crumbs of rumor."[5]

In the course of time, God restores Job's fortunes with a new family and new wealth. This time, Job doesn't ask why.

What if God flips our *why* questions back around on us, just as Jesus flipped the tables in the Temple courts?

What if he confronted us with his own divine list of *whys*?

Why didn't you listen to me?
Why didn't you see the signs?
Why didn't you do what I said?

What kind of weak excuses would we offer?

I didn't hear you.
I was tired.
I did the best I could.

Often, we impose our answers on God. We accuse him of not hearing our prayers. We think he's tired of helping us. Or that he did the best he could (which, sadly, wasn't enough).

What kind of God is that?

Certainly not one worthy of our worship.

His answers are different from the ones we expect when we ask the question. It's never that he's too tired to answer—it's that he's too kind.

"I AM" is a short answer—with lo-o-ong implications—from a worthy God.

KNOWING *WHY* DOESN'T CHANGE ANYTHING

In the question-filled Gospel of John, Jesus and his students encounter a man born blind. The obvious question is *why*? The common Jewish perception was that sickness came as a direct result of sin, either personal or generational. The ancient doctrine of retribution stipulated that goodness produced goodness; badness produced badness. This view was reinforced by certain passages in the Hebrew scriptures.[6]

So Jesus' followers ask, "Why is he blind? Who sinned? Was it this man or his parents?"

Because we all reap what we sow, they wanted to know *who sowed*?

This same question has perplexed people for as long as we have ventured to talk to God.

Who's to blame?

Jesus responds, "It is neither about his sin or his parents' sin. This has happened so that God can demonstrate his power."[7]

Jesus is more inclined to act than to answer. Instead of

explaining the unexplainable, Jesus simply fixes the problem. He heals the man.

One minute he's blind; the next minute he sees perfectly. No explanation, no commentary, no grandstanding. Jesus simply acts.

The Rabbi's message? Instead of asking, "Why is there evil and sickness in the world?" fix the problem!

Knowing *why* something happened doesn't change *what* happened. If we know the reason why our spouse died of lung cancer, it still doesn't bring him or her back to life. It doesn't make our grief any less. Yes, but knowing *why* may allow for changes in the future. If Daddy died of lung cancer caused by smoking, it might prevent little Johnny from picking up a cigarette.

We are dead serious about the *why* prayer. Clearly, there are times when *why* is an important question—not to change the past, but potentially to change the future. "Why, God?" can be heart driven, an emotionally loaded plea heaved up from the gut. Something ominous happens, and we want to assign the blame. We want reasons. We want an explanation.

Some of our *why* questions are as old as life itself:

> Why is there evil?
> Why do bad things happen to good people?
> Why does a good God allow such pain and suffering?

But *why* can easily move beyond an honest request to become a passive-aggressive demand for reparation. It can ring with a scolding tone, expecting God to own up to some grand foible and concede that he's done something wrong.

We attempt to lay our grievances at his doorstep, but God stoutly refuses to be made answerable for the mishaps of this world. He is God, and he won't take responsibility for that which he didn't do. God won't be made party to evil. It is in the world of its own accord. God won't be made to feel the guilt.

But the Bible never explains evil. The lack of explanation drives us toward our own logical conclusions when we can't find God's rationale. Either God is all-powerful and unjust, or he's just, but too weak to enforce his justice.

The ancient Jews answered the perplexity differently. For them, the solution was both/and. It says in the Psalms, "One thing God has spoken, two things have I heard; that you, O God, are strong, and that you, O Lord, are loving."[8] We see the issue as a dichotomy: powerful and unjust, or just and weak. But for God, it is a unified question. He is loving *and* strong. The psalmist's answer forces us to reconsider our own. Sometimes we can't see the answer because it isn't obvious until we ask a different question.

Framing the Question

There is a legend in Greek literature about a local strongman named Hieron, who commissioned a goldsmith to forge a crown in the shape of a laurel wreath. Hieron suspected the goldsmith had substituted silver for a portion of the gold, but he couldn't prove it. So Hieron hired Archimedes, a mathematician/physician/engineer to solve the mystery.

This presented Archimedes with a dilemma. How could he assess the purity of the metal without damaging the work of art? He could melt it down and measure the density as a cube. But that would be destroying the crown to spite the smith. There had to be another way.

New solutions follow new questions.

One day, Archimedes visited the city's public baths. When he climbed into the pool, he noticed that the farther his body sank into the water, the more the water poured out onto the floor.

Then he asked a curious question: "How much water?" The solution came suddenly. Of course! The volume of the overflowing water would exactly equal the volume of his body.

Instantly, Archimedes linked this insight to his perplexity with Hieron's crown: Gold weighs more than silver. A crown with silver alloy would have to be bulkier to reach the same weight as one of pure gold; therefore, it would displace more water.

"Aha!"

Elated with his own genius, the young Greek scientist bounded out of his bath and streaked home crying, "Eureka!" Archimedes had discovered the foundational principle of displacement. It is probably legend, but the 2,250-year-old tale of a Greek mathematician running naked down the street screaming "Eureka!" makes a good story.

History leaps forward in the wake of "aha!" moments. When we ask new questions, and we get a fresh view of the situation, solutions appear where none were before. Experience shows us that when we're stuck, instead of grinding the old question into finer and finer dust, swapping the old question for a new one leads to revelation.

Is that why Jesus so often answered tired old questions with fresh new ones?

Johannes Gutenberg claimed that the idea of the movable-type printing press came "like a ray of light" after he asked, "What would make pressing paper and ink faster?"

Einstein's theory of relativity hit him like a thunderclap during a thought experiment with the quirky question, "What if I rode on a light beam?"

Instead of merely rubbing his bruised noggin and taking a bite out of the apple, Sir Isaac Newton asked, "How did that happen?"

New questions birth new perspectives. Since there is no way to reduce the answer of "Why, God?" into something digestible to the human mind, what if we swap out the old question for a new one?

Prayers asking *why* are a postmortem review. *Why* doesn't change the past and is rarely important in the present.

An emergency room doctor doesn't have time to sort out causes. She has to save a life. Why a car ran a red light is of little immediate concern. She simply needs to know how to stabilize the breathing of the accident victim. The first question in the wake of an emergency is *what* or *how*, not *why*. Even "Why is the patient bleeding?" becomes secondary to "How do we stop the bleeding?"

Why is important only as it informs future behavior. There will be plenty of time throughout eternity to sort out the bits and pieces of causation into perfect and understandable order. In the meantime, we must get busy and stop the bleeding.

Perhaps there is a spiritual application here.

WHY TO HOW

When we turn from *why* to *how*, God seems ready and willing to accommodate us. *How* might be as far as we get with God.

"How do I stop the grieving?"

"How do I live my life now?"

"How do I translate your heart into this situation?"

Jesus had a mission statement for his time on earth. It was a plan to rescue the world. The plan was foretold by Isaiah in an ancient prophecy. Jesus retells the plan in his own words in the Gospel of Luke:

> The Spirit of the LORD is upon me, for he has anointed me to bring Good News to the poor. He has sent me to proclaim that captives will be released, that the blind will see, that the oppressed will be set free, and that the time of the LORD's favor has come.[9]

This is Jesus announcing ahead of time the business he will attend to. He will provide for the poor, pardon the guilty, heal the broken, deliver those in the grip of evil, and give favor to everyone who will receive it. And this is precisely what he does. Faced with troubling encounters on every page of the Gospels, Jesus moves on the offensive—and when he does, situations are transformed for the better. He fixes things. He ignores the *why* and moves on to the *how*.

How do we translate *why* to *how*?

Maybe it's not, "Why was my son killed by a drunken driver?" but "How can I keep this from happening to someone else's son?"

Instead of, "Why didn't you answer my prayer?" maybe it's, "How did I miss your answer?"

What if "Why can't I?" became "How can I?"

Maybe the very situations that bring us to the *why* question aren't meant to leave us there. Maybe they're supposed to take us somewhere else.

Maybe asking *why* prepares our hearts, provides insight, and gives us the necessary experience to then drop the *why* and—with God's help—pick up the holy *how*.

If there isn't a satisfactory answer to the question of *why*, then why ask it?

God solves problems.

He doesn't resolve *why*s.

He asks us to do the same.

HOW'S THAT FOR UNDERSTANDING?

If the answer to *why* is incomprehensible to us in both its short and long forms, *how* is completely knowable. Maybe not right now, maybe not all at once, but with *how* there is the potential to discover at least the next step.

Michael, barefoot and pajama-clad, trotted into the kitchen. His every-which-way hair bore witness to how deeply he had slept the previous night. His greeting that morning was straight to the point: "Dad, the light burned out. I need a new one."

Upon waking, Michael had flipped on the light to find his slippers, but the bulb had flashed and burned out. No problem. He knew where the light came from—his dad. Together, they walked to the storage room, and his father selected a new bulb. With Michael trotting behind in his bare feet, Dad led the way to the little boy's room.

Two minutes later, the old bulb was out and the new one screwed in place. Michael hit the switch, and *voilà!* Seeing a teaching moment, his dad asked, "Hey Michael, do you have any idea why this works?"

"Sure," Michael said, flipping the switch off and on again three or four times. "Because of this."

Michael found his slippers near the end of his bed. "Thanks, Dad," he said as he headed toward the kitchen for a bowl of toasted oats.

Michael didn't need to know the details of how electricity is generated. He didn't care to know how the juice from some distant power plant traveled over miles of wires to his house. He didn't ponder how the hairlike filament inside the vacuum bulb turned the current to light. He only knew that when he saw his father twist a bulb into the socket and when he flipped the switch, the darkness in his room disappeared.

But just because Michael doesn't completely understand how it works, he doesn't consider it magic. He knows there is a commonsense, down-to-earth reason for all this. But he doesn't concern himself with *why* it works; he simply knows *how* to make it work.

We're not much different as adults. Except for the rare genius among us, few grasp the complex physics behind the phenomenon of electricity. When the sun goes down at the end of the day, we just flip the switch. Successful living means a whole lot more than scientific explanation. As long as we consistently perform an action that ends in a consistent result, that's typically all the proof we need— even for Edison, whose lightbulb worked for years before physicists could articulate the wave and particle theories of light.

Understanding how to get something to work seems infinitely more important than why it works. This is true of electricity, but what if it's also true of divinity? Knowing *how*

God's heart is moved could be more important than knowing *why*.

Why is a desire for rationality and order; but to our limited understanding, God isn't always rational or comprehensible.

Our relationship with God can easily handle confrontation, even when we ask why. But *why* is a prayer God can never answer in a way that we can comprehend, any more than a pregnant woman can fully answer "Why is there a baby in your tummy?" for a curious four-year-old. The full answer includes complexity, mystery, and things we're not yet ready to handle.

Perhaps in eternity, with a million-billion years to spare, we'll be able to understand *why* if we choose to sit and read all the files of our lives and factor in the influence of all those butterfly effects, until it is comprehensible in one whole, unified picture, a picture of Everything.

Then again, maybe not.

Maybe we will never know *why* because we will never be God.

KEEP ON ASKING

It's frustrating to think that *why* is the prayer to which we'll rarely get an answer. But it's not because God wants us to stop asking. He just wants us to stop demanding an answer on our own terms.

Why leads us to God, not through an explanation of circumstances, but through the path it takes to get us to him. His silence isn't meant to frustrate us but to bring us closer.

Pediatrician Alan Greene has a theory about toddlers'

infatuation with the question *why*. His insight suggests something profound about the passion that drives all human curiosity.

> I've found that, when I try to answer children at this stage of development with the reason for something, they are left cold. After conversing with thousands of children, I've decided that what they really mean is, "That's interesting to me. Let's talk about that together." . . .
>
> I remember when one of my own sons asked me why the sky was blue. I told him that on sunny days the sky was blue and that on cloudy days it was gray and that at night it was very, very dark. Sometimes, in between day and night, it's a pretty pink or orange. . . . He was delighted.[10]

According to Dr. Greene, *why* from a child is not so much a quest for pure knowledge as a tease for conversation. The child who asks "But why?" after being commanded to bed isn't interested in a dissertation, but in stalling for time and squeezing out a thimbleful more of attention from a hurried parent.

Maybe that's what we want from God too.

Could it be that when we aim for answers to *why* we miss the target of the relationship?

Our goal is to answer a question. Perhaps God has a different goal. Maybe more than answers, he wants more questions. When we lack satisfactory answers in this world, we're driven to look outside of ourselves for deeper meaning.

The fact that we ask *why* so often, and God so rarely answers, is by design. A sort of spiritual homing device to help us find the target. While we're getting frustrated at missing the bull's-eye, God is reloading our ammunition and hoping that sooner or later we'll see we're aiming in the wrong direction.

If so, it seems that God isn't like a parent who wants to end all *why*s with a "because I said so." Instead, he might actually encourage our *why*s—for a greater purpose.

So why ask *why* even when God rarely answers it?

Why not?

5
RAPISTS, MURDERERS, AND "WHY DOES HE GET TO SIT NEXT TO THE WINDOW?"
Prayers for Justice

FEW PLACES ON EARTH are as tempestuous as Yellowstone in winter. There, the steaming ire of the earth and the anger of the skies collide. From above, monster storms crush the surrounding mountains with as much as six feet of snow in a mere three days. Below, festering cauldrons of mud and geysers of fire and water burst forth from earth's molten core, melting the snow and ice, even when the air temperature falls to sixty degrees below zero. Yellowstone is simultaneously a world of icy bitterness and sulfurous, rank heat. It is a place where the earth's brooding and violent passions lose constraint and bubble to the surface—set into motion by the restless force of energy.

We are a part of this same conflicted earth.

THE SMELL OF INJUSTICE
We're born with fully developed injustice sensors. We can sniff out unfairness from the first time someone divides

a cookie and gives us the smaller half. At that age, maybe two or three, our vocabulary is limited, but words aren't even necessary. Our tears scream, "That's not fair!" just as eloquently.

But as we grow, our vocabulary and our ability to detect injustice increase.

> "She got more!"
> "He cheated!"
> "I was here first."
> "You like him better."
> "That's mine."
> "Hers is bigger."
> "He got to pick last time."
> "She's on my side of the boardroom."

This isn't learned behavior—toddlers don't grow up watching Mommy and Daddy fight over who got the larger cup of coffee. It's inbred. Our sense of righteousness, our desire for justice, is in the package we receive at birth. We're hardwired to recognize what's fair and what's not. And to complain loudly when it's not.

In a violent neighborhood in North Minneapolis, Alywyn Foster opens the gym doors of Hospitality House at 3:00 p.m. Thirty minutes later, the place is packed with kids looking for a warm, safe, and welcoming place to hang out. Foster sets up just off center court. He calls the kids by name. "Eddie! Hey . . . none of that!" But mostly, the kids referee their own games. Foster steps in only when things get rough. His role is something of a cross between big brother, county court judge, boxing referee, and school vice principal.

"That was a foul!" shouts Alec.

"No way!" argues Eddie.

"You fouled me. Now give me the ball," insists Alec.

They stand toe to toe. Their argument is telling. Neither denies the existence of fouls or whether fouls should be overlooked. Every twelve-year-old knows that a foul is a foul, and that basketball wouldn't exist without some established set of standards. What Eddie and Alec scuffle over is whether *that* particular elbow to the ribs was a foul.

Justice and injustice are a given, and every kid knows the bottom line—even those raised on the streets, where justice so often seems perverted. That's why pickup games, even in the most unruly neighborhoods, are remarkably self-contained. Alywyn Foster is simply there to teach the rules, not to create an awareness that there are rules.

Paul of Tarsus, the first public broadcaster of Christian ideas, wrote in a letter to believers living in Rome that the concept of right and wrong is written into the heart of every human being. Everyone, he said, has justice encoded.[1] It's like a preference for pretty faces or broad shoulders; it's part of our genetic code.

The ancient Hebrews didn't stand around discussing the merits of justice; they simply prayed for it to come.

Jeremiah took his case directly to God. "LORD, you always give me justice when I bring a case before you. So let me bring you this complaint: Why are the wicked so prosperous? Why are evil people so happy?"[2]

The Hebrews prayed this way because they believed God cared deeply about righteousness. The prophet Amos rampaged through the streets crying out on behalf of God,

"I want to see a mighty flood of justice, an endless river of righteous living."[3]

Amos's oracle was a cry for justice.

What do our cries for justice look like?

"It's not fair!"
"Did you see what he did to me?"
"It's my turn."

In adult terms, our prayers might sound something like

"What did I do to deserve that?"
"He should be locked up for life!"
"Why doesn't somebody do something about that?"

Like Jeremiah, are we provoked to pray when we see injustice? Could our cries for a remedy, our desire for things to be righted, actually be in response to God?

Provoked to Prayer

Often we're provoked to prayer, not because of the situation itself but because of the emotion that rises within us.

The same energy that lies deep below the surface of Yellowstone is reminiscently similar to the wild, untamed passion that bubbles under our calm, civilized facades. Usually, this molten fury lies buried deep in our cores, capped off by resolute egos that diligently guard us from the dangers of our own impulses. But at certain places and times, at the "Yellowstone moments" of our lives, our passions burst through.

When we want the murderer sentenced to life in prison,

the thief punished, the hostile driver ticketed, the insolent child scolded, or the gossiper called on the carpet, not only are we recognizing the injustice, we're provoked to anger by the situation.

We have varying thermostats. Our anger can be awakened unexpectedly by a spouse who breaks a promise, a driver who cuts in front of us during rush-hour traffic, or a neighborhood bully who threatens our child. A spark of anger ignites within us and fuels the flames, turning our careful constraints into a wide-sweeping, fast-moving, and dangerous inferno.

We lose control.

One petty injustice awakens something in us wilder and far more powerful than our own self-control.

When injustice unleashes our anger, the emotional eruption means that a line has been crossed, a standard has been broken. But could our anger be more than just an emotion? Could it be a sign of moral health?

Like a fever signals an infection, maybe our anger signals that the proper order of things has been compromised. There's a problem to address. And often we want to address it ourselves.

At some point, every breathing human has tasted the toxic desire for revenge. When justice doesn't come on its own, we're not above taking matters into our own hands. Interactive Web sites like www.thepayback.com provide tools for victims plotting and executing retaliation against wrongs suffered. Our passion to make things right often drives us to the point of personal retaliation and vengeance.

A wrong.

Anger.

Revenge.

How could these things bring us closer to God?

In *Mere Christianity*, C. S. Lewis claims that moral judgments, evident in the anger we feel over a wrong suffered, are perhaps the strongest argument for the existence of a moral God.

If God is a God of justice, and if we're made in his image, perhaps our anger is more than an emotional reaction.

Maybe it is a movement toward God.

When rage raises its demanding head and grabs the wheel of our lives, we may feel farthest from God. We feel anything but spiritual. But is it possible that these are the very moments when we are closest to—and maybe even the most like—God?

Justice matters to us, but it also matters to God. Perhaps that is why we instinctively cry out to him when we experience injustice.

APPEALING TO AUTHORITY

As children, when we saw injustice, we appealed to a higher authority to fix things:

> "Mom, his piece is bigger than mine."
> "Dad, he got to sit by the window the last time."
> "Mrs. Moseley, he's kicking me."

Perhaps that explains why we continue to appeal to a higher power when injustice happens to us as adults. When we can't exact the outcome we feel so passionate about, when we don't have a way to carry it out, we appeal to a power greater than ourselves in the form of a parent, teacher, boss, neighborhood-watch group, court system, federal government, or local Mafia boss. We call on them to administer justice on our behalf. From the time we're kids, we recognize that justice comes from outside sources, so when we aren't satisfied by the systems of the world, we appeal to the Highest Authority of all.

For justice's sake, we pray. "God, it's just not fair!"

We understand that God cares about big injustices in the world—things like the Holocaust, perhaps—but we often forget that God is also concerned about seemingly petty injustices. In fact, Jesus was angry enough to curse when he thought things weren't as they should be.

Jesus curses

You might not hear about it in a Sunday morning sermon, but Jesus cursed. And, from our modern perspective, he seems to have had a rather wimpy reason. It's almost as if he walked into a store and discovered they were out of the one item he wanted, or a restaurant closed just as he arrived. In short, Jesus got ticked off because he was *hungry*.

Matthew describes the event in his Gospel. Matthew was a tax collector—the ancient counterpart of an IRS agent— before he became a disciple. He was familiar with collecting a percentage of the yield from local citizens, and not much escaped him. He knew how to account for produce.

Here's how he describes the event: Jesus was returning to the city, and he was hungry. He saw a fig tree and looked forward to some nice, juicy fruit. But the tree didn't have any fruit, only leaves. Matthew reports that Jesus then cursed the tree, saying something along the lines of "No more figs from this tree—ever!"

95

Essentially, Jesus damns the tree from ever producing more fruit.

So what happens to the tree?

It withers on the spot. Matthew and the other witnesses agree it dried up to little more than a stick.[4]

Pretty impressive, huh?

Wouldn't we like to have the power to call upon the name of God to obliterate those who've wronged us—well, at least until we've cooled down?

Those who witnessed the event were dumbfounded. "How did you do that?" they wanted to know.

The fig tree was a symbol of the Hebrew people who professed to believe God but failed to produce action. Jesus' curse was more than a condemnation of a fruitless tree. It was a prayer for righteousness.

"You can do this," Jesus said to the witnesses.

No doubt they were listening intently to what came next.

"In fact," Jesus said, "you can do even more. You can tell a mountain to jump into the sea, and it will lift up and come crashing down in the water. You just need to have faith. With faith, you can pray for anything. Big or small. And you'll get it."

This isn't the first example of a man calling on God's power to curse those who had wronged him. A thousand years before Jesus, King David used song prayers to call down a curse on his enemies. "O God, if only you would destroy the wicked! Get out of my life, you murderers!"[5] And again, "Let the wicked be disgraced; let them lie silent in the grave."[6] In his frustration to see justice, David audaciously cries out to God to "kill 'em all!"

Hmm. Being able to call down the wrath of God on the

woman putting on her makeup while driving the car ahead of us would be pretty satisfying. But that's the problem, isn't it? When we're left to administer our own justice, we tend to pervert it.

PERVERTING JUSTICE

On an episode of the television show *Studio 60 on the Sunset Strip*, the character Jack Randolph says, "Thieves get rich and saints get shot, and God doesn't answer prayers a lot." Though believers may disagree on the frequency with which God answers prayer, they still understand Randolph's sentiments, especially when they cry out for righteousness in a world that often seems unjust.

If God is a God of justice, and by his very nature he must bring righteousness, then why don't we see his response to our prayers?

If God *always* answers our prayers for justice, it must be that he answers them differently than we expect or desire.

What we really want when we cry out for justice is for God to exact revenge for us, isn't it? We want him to answer our prayers with the same vengeance with which we spewed them out.

He rarely seems to do this.

A pious but cranky old woman was perturbed because her neighbors forgot to invite her to their picnic. On the morning of the event, they suddenly realized their oversight and sent a little boy to ask her to attend. "It's too late now," she snapped. "I've already prayed for rain."

Perhaps our prayers for justice are like the old woman's prayer—shortsighted and mean-spirited. Not only are we hoping for the ruin of someone else's picnic, but we're also calling thunderclouds down on our own heads.

What if God were to *get us* for the same offenses we want him to get others? This heavenly tit-for-tat could play out with unintended consequences. We get a flat tire right after cutting off someone in traffic. We spit our gum out the window and later step in someone else's discarded wad in the office parking lot. We laugh at others' misfortunes only to find them laughing at ours.

What if when we said "damn it" or "damn you," we were actually inviting God to damn us? Perhaps we don't really want justice if it means we get it ourselves as well.

But is it really better to hold our position at any cost? Insisting on our own justice can cost us dearly.

Fifty-two-year-old Robert Smith walked slowly down the sidewalk, leaning on his cane to aid his ailing foot. On the same side of the sidewalk, walking toward him on her way to the bank, was seventy-six-year-old Walberga Schaller and her cane. Like a slow-motion train wreck, both Smith and Schaller believed they had the right of way. They moved forward until they were only inches apart. Insults escalated to obscenities, and then they began clubbing each other with their canes. When it was over, Walberga Schaller was sprawled on the sidewalk, and Robert Smith faced assault charges.[7] Justice was ultimately granted by an outside source.

Biblical mediation is the process of two people agreeing to follow biblical principles to work out a dispute. An eager attorney, initially excited by the possibilities this held for solving legal disputes, couldn't wait to implement the process in his practice.

Several years later, the attorney abandoned the idea, disappointed by how many clients used the Bible as a basis for arguing their personal point of view rather than agreeing on a solution. Entrenched in their respective positions, both sides refused to give up any ground in the dispute, even though holding that ground meant agreeing to theological views inconsistent with traditional biblical teaching. Their sense of justice overwhelmed their understanding of other biblical concepts such as grace, mercy, and love.

The desire to hang on even if we're wrong is what happens when our intuitive sense of justice becomes distorted. Perhaps even perverted. Intellectually, we know right from wrong, but faced with our own emotional involvement, we often insist on holding others to a higher standard of justice than we expect from ourselves.

Exacting our own revenge can be devastating. Though it may taste sweet for a moment, in time, it turns bitter and eats at the soul.

In Shakespeare's *The Merchant of Venice*, Shylock, a Jewish moneylender, is treacherously betrayed by two Christians, Salanio and Salarino. In a fierce speech on revenge, Shylock swears to return their evil with his own evil. "The villainy you teach me I will execute," he rages. Toward the end of his speech, almost like a refrain, he chants the word *revenge*.

For a moment, we're sympathetic to Shylock's cause. We feel the injustice and understand his hostility. But then Shakespeare turns the focus onto Shylock himself. We learn that in his drive for justice, he has become obsessed. Corrupted with hatred and greed, he is unable to love anything but riches. Even his daughter, Jessica, means

99

nothing to him. "I would my daughter were dead at my foot, and the jewels in her ear!"[8] Shylock's desire for justice is so strong that it has twisted him with a violent and horrific hatred. We can see it, but he cannot.

The perversion of justice also reigns as the theme of Alexandre Dumas' novel *The Count of Monte Cristo*. Edmond Dantes lives a blessed life. At the age of nineteen, he becomes captain of the ship *Pharaon*, is set to marry his beautiful fiancée, Mercedes, and has won the favor of some powerful men.

But Dantes's good fortune inspires jealousy in those he considers friends. These men conspire to ruin Dantes by accusing him of being a Bonapartist. As a result, he is arrested and sentenced to life in an isolated island prison.

After years in solitary confinement, Dantes sinks into despair until he meets Abbé Faria, a fellow prisoner and Italian priest. His hope is renewed. Faria educates Dantes, helps him sort out the mysterious details of his betrayal, and confides in Dantes the location of a great treasure hidden on the island of Monte Cristo. After Faria's death, Dantes escapes and sets out to find the treasure. He reinvents himself as the Count of Monte Cristo, a mysterious and fabulously wealthy aristocrat.

Ten years after his return to Marseilles, Dantes begins his plan to avenge his enemies and reward the few who remained faithful to him. One by one he destroys the fortunes, families, and lives of his foes. But as his own mode of justice unfolds, Dantes finds his efforts to mete out rewards and punishments have become impossibly intertwined. Those he favors and those he opposes have intricate relationships with one another. When he rewards a friend, he unwittingly rewards a foe. When he punishes an enemy, he accidentally punishes a friend. He finally comes to renounce his role as an agent of God's vengeance. Only after he relinquishes this bitter mission to the sovereignty of God is he free to begin a new life of love and hope.

"Revenge," said Albert Schweitzer, "is like a rolling stone, which, when a man hath forced up a hill, will return upon him with a greater violence, and break those bones whose sinews gave it motion."[9]

Our inherent *desire* for fairness is so strong that it can blind us to what real justice looks like. This would explain why biblical mediation fails even among the willing. Both parties want fairness so much that they can't separate their desire for equality to discover what justice looks like for their situation. They hold fast to their claims of fairness at the expense of finding a just solution.

It happens to all of us in varying degrees. We believe we have the right of way because we're late for a dental appointment, but perhaps the other driver is on his way to the hospital with a wife in labor.

God's justice is so absolute that he's passed that sense of fairness on to his creation, even if we can't see it.

Fortunately, God sees all.

He rarely answers our cries for justice with our suggested outcomes. Instead of advancing the scenarios we desire, he reinforces our *desire*—for fairness, equality, righteousness, and justice. No wonder our passions are so strong! Even when we're wrong, our *sense* of righteousness only increases.

Could it be that one way he answers our prayers is to take our passion, our anger, our innate sense of fairness and ask us to turn it over to him? to allow him to execute perfect justice?

The Hebrew scriptures often equate God with justice:

- "The LORD is known for his justice."[10]
- "The righteous LORD loves justice."[11]
- "Everything he does is just and fair."[12]
- "The LORD is a God of justice."[13]

God cares about justice, and he personally experiences the pain of injustices in the world. God is no neutral bystander.

The emotion of anger by itself isn't the problem. The problem comes when we believe we know the *just* outcome. But we can't ever know what is the best course of action—what is truly just—because we aren't God.

His nature means that he must also be the administrator of justice: "When I sharpen my flashing sword and begin to carry out justice, I will take revenge on my enemies and repay those who reject me."[14]

The Jewish philosopher Abraham J. Heschel believes that the standard of justice is not some abstract exemplar, but rather the very voice of God.

> Justice is not an ancient custom, a human convention, a value, but a transcendent demand, freighted with divine concern. It is not only a relationship between man and man, it is an *act* involving God, a divine need. . . . It is not one of His ways, but in all of His ways. Its validity is not only universal, but also eternal. . . .

God's concern for justice grows out of His compassion for man. The prophets do not speak of a divine relationship to an absolute principle or idea, called justice. They are intoxicated with the awareness of God's relationship with His people and to all men.[15]

Like God, we need to move beyond the anger to feel the *pain* of injustice.

Gary A. Haugen is president of the International Justice Mission in Washington, D.C. As director of the United Nations genocide investigation in Rwanda in 1994, Haugen's job was to sort through dead bodies and collect evidence of the crimes that took place in an effort to prosecute the offenders. In his book *Good News About Injustice*, he gives an account of his time there:

> In Rwanda, where I had to bear the burden of digging through the twisted, reeking, remains of horrific mass graves, I tried to imagine, for just a minute, what it must have been like for God to be present at each of the massacre sites as thousands of Tutsi women and children were murdered. Frankly, the idea was impossible to bear. But the thought led me to imagine what it must be like for God to be present, this year, at the rape of all the world's child prostitutes, at the beatings of all the world's prisoners of conscience, at the moment the last breath of hope expires from the breast of each of the millions of small children languishing in bonded servitude. As I would approach my God in prayer, I could hear his gentle voice say to me, "Son, do you have any idea where your Father has been lately?"[16]

Like God, we need to feel the pain; but God, unlike us, has a holy anger and a perfect sense of justice.

THE REAL AIM OF INJUSTICE

There are horrific examples of injustice throughout history. In Rome, early Christians were sent into stadiums to be eaten by lions for sport. Women thought to be witches were burned to death in the early days of America. Men were hanged in the South because of the color of their skin. Jews and many others faced unimaginable persecution and death at the hands of the Nazis.

As children we hear of these things and ask, "How could anyone let that happen?"

Then we grow up to watch the Rwandan crisis on the news while we eat dinner.

We're naïve enough to think slavery no longer exists, though statistics show that there are more slaves now than at any other time in history.

Poverty doesn't make us angry; it makes us sad.

Childhood prostitution seems like something that happens in other countries, and it does. Every day. To hundreds of thousands of children, just like ours. But it also happens in our country.

But instead of feeling the pain of injustice in our world, we get upset because we didn't get the larger piece, because a car cut us off in traffic, because we didn't get what we felt we deserved. Somehow, our well-functioning justice detectors have missed their targets.

Perhaps our own experiences with injustice are about something more than righting wrongs. Perhaps they're about getting right with the one who is righteous.

Long ago, in the days of Israel's divided kingdom, 750 years before the birth of Jesus, there lived a prudish, upright bachelor-hermit named Hosea. Hosea was known in Israel as a marginal mystic. He experienced trances and dreams and announced them to the world as the word of the Lord. Hosea was a prophet.

At the time, the religion of Canaan was a fertility cult that linked the land's fruitfulness to the marital bliss of gods and goddesses. When the male god Baal and his female consort, Asherah, were intimate, the land produced crops. The worship of Baal and Asherah at local shrines became an ongoing orgy. Male and female prostitutes joined in erotic acts with worshipers to stimulate the gods and make the land fertile. By the time of Hosea, Canaanite worship had polluted Israel's worship of God.

Against this cultural backdrop, God presented Hosea with a special, though pitiable, assignment. "Go find a young Hebrew woman. Woo her. Love her. And marry her."

For a bachelor like Hosea, those must have been exciting and terrifying words, especially as God continued, "But I warn you, if you love her, as you must, she will break your heart and leave you for another. Now go."

Hosea obeyed.

Stepping outside the walls of his cloistered life, he found and fell passionately in love with a young, promiscuous party girl named Gomer. He won her hand, married her, and brought her back to the safety of his home. There they began a family together, raising three children.

Time passed. We're not told how much. But eventually God's dire warning came true. Gomer left Hosea and her children and returned to her wild ways. It broke Hosea's heart.

Gomer was typical of the young women in her culture. She was a liberated worshiper of Asherah, religiously faithful to the fertility cult. But under Hosea's roof, she was restrained from her promiscuity. Ultimately, she was drawn back to what she had known.

God again approached Hosea. "Now you know," he said. "You know how I feel. I loved my people. I was married to them and passionately enthralled by them. But they have forgotten me."

So, in chapter two of the book of *Hosea*, we see the Creator of the universe and Hosea, this poor, broken man, sitting on the equivalent of a modern-day front porch and having a long cry together. They understand each other's pain—the bitterness of injustice.

Misery loves company . . . because it needs company.

As two jilted lovers dry their tears and wipe their noses, God turns to Hosea and says, "Go get her. Bring her back. And love her again."

Hosea listens, because this is what God is doing. He, too, has loved and been rejected, but his love never fails, and he chooses to give his heart away knowing he will be rejected again.

Hosea goes out into the streets and finds Gomer. She's in bondage, having sold herself into temple prostitution. Hosea buys her freedom, though it costs him everything. He must barter away his own food for the balance of her bill.

He takes her home. Again.

Could it be that the injustices we experience, the anger and heartbrokenness we feel, bring us closer to God?

When Gary Haugen returned home from his Rwandan

investigation, he was disappointed that friends in his Washington, D.C., suburb weren't more interested in what he'd been through. His experiences in Africa left his relationships at home feeling a little shallow. However, his closest friends insisted that he talk about his time in Rwanda so they could better understand how the experience had affected him. Gary equates this desire to understand with our relationship to God:

> Likewise if we really want to know God, we should know something about where he has been—and what it has been like for him to suffer with all those who are hurting and abused. No one will ever *really* know what it was like for me to interview all those orphaned massacre survivors in Rwanda or to roll back a corpse in a Rwandan church and find the tiniest of skeletons under the remains of a mother who had tried to protect her baby with her own body. I would never expect people to totally understand. God doesn't expect this either. He knows we can never comprehend the smallest fraction of oppression and abuse that he has had to witness. But we can know him better if we try to understand something about his character and experience as the God of compassion—the God who suffers with the victims of injustice.
>
> If nothing else, it will help us understand why the God of justice *hates* injustice and wants it to stop. If we had to see and hear it every day like our God does, we would hate it too. To understand where the God of compassion has been is to begin to understand God's passion for justice.[17]

For a minute, Hosea got a glimpse of what it felt like to be God. Gary Haugen asks us to do the same, and it is our own experiences of injustice that help us transition from our own feelings to God's.

The story of Hosea shows us that God is personally moved by any experience of broken trust and that whenever we have hated injustice, we have been like God. This partnership in pain is itself a form of answer to our prayers. To know God, to hear his answer, means being thrown into the teeth of love. It means volunteering our hearts to be broken over unrighteousness. But it also means that we can sit with him as a friend and share his tears.

Enough, Already. Do Something!

God personally feels injustice.

He feels the pain of broken promises.

But does he ever hear and actually respond to our appeals for justice by moving to fix the problem in real time?

If God is just and powerful, it is natural for us to assume that he is able to intervene and fix any injustice he chooses. We might even blame him if he doesn't immediately fix things. To us, this may seem an entirely new injustice. "Do something!" we pray.

Jesus told a story about a woman who brought her case for justice before a crooked judge.[18] Though her case seemed reasonable, this official was not inclined to offer her a hearing, probably because she couldn't afford to pay a bribe. But the woman would not be silenced. She continued to present her case. Again and again she returned for a ruling. Finally, because of her persistence and in spite of his lack of honor, the judge agreed to her appeal.

Jesus uses this story to exhort us to appeal to God in prayer for justice. If a crooked judge will respond to persistence, how much more will our God, who is perfectly fair, respond to our prayers to remedy injustices?

Yes, God acts here and now in response to our prayers.

But beyond feeling our pain, does he provide real answers to our divine appeals?

There is an ancient story of a king who wished to settle accounts with his servants. The first debtor owed him ten thousand talents, an amount that is almost beyond calculation. When the debtor tells the king he is unable to pay, his master orders him to be sold as a slave. The debtor pleads for patience and promises to repay. The king's response, however, is more than merciful; he completely releases the man and forgives his debt, bearing the entire loss himself.

The same servant then confronts a man who owes him a small debt. Like the king, he demands the debtor pay what he owes. This second debtor pleads for mercy and asks for time to repay. But instead of showing the kindness he was shown, the first man refuses mercy to the second.

When the king learns of this, he is furious. He says to the first debtor, "I forgave you because you begged me. You should have shown the same to this man." In a twist of justice, the king then retracts his forgiveness and jails the first debtor.[19]

The meaning of the parable is vivid. The king cares about justice. He is also merciful in his response. His mercy is boundless, even when he has to bear the price of the debt himself.

As you probably guessed, the ancient storyteller who first told this parable was Jesus. And he related it just a few days before he suffered the darkest injustice any human has ever experienced. Blameless and sinless, he took the punishment for all of the sins of the world—past, present, and future—to the cross, forgiving those who heaped their iniquities upon him.

Justice is real and necessary. But in response to our pleas, Jesus asks, "Do you really want justice? Do you want this standard applied to your life without the balance of mercy?" He reminds us that the standard we use against others will be the standard God will use against us.

Reciprocity and Release

God's favor is conditioned upon reciprocity. This idea parallels Jesus' teaching on prayer and forgiveness in Matthew 6:14-15. There, in summing up his teaching about prayer, Jesus boldly lays out a condition: "If you forgive those who sin against you, your heavenly Father will forgive you. But if you refuse to forgive others, your Father will not forgive your sins."

By extending mercy and releasing justice into God's hands, we allow God to liberate us from the exacting demands of justice. We find mercy in him. When we cry for forgiveness, God answers by forgiving the injustices we have released into the world. If we leave our desire for justice in God's hands and permit him to level the score in his own time and in his own way, we can stand free, both of the demands justice makes of us and of the bitterness of the injustices we have suffered.

After nineteen years of imprisonment for stealing food for his starving family, the peasant Jean Valjean is released. Rejected by innkeepers who do not want to take in a convict, Valjean sleeps on the street until the benevolent Bishop Myriel takes him in and gives him shelter. In the night, Valjean steals the bishop's silverware and runs. He is caught, but the bishop rescues him by claiming that the silver was a gift. The bishop then tells him that, in exchange, he must become an honest man.

The rest of the story follows Jean Valjean as he seeks to live a life of mercy in response to the mercies he has been shown, though he can never escape the scars of his past. In the end, however, he is vindicated, and his commitment to a life of mercy is rewarded. Victor Hugo's novel, *Les Misérables*, portrays the pains and rewards of living a life of mercy in response to bitter injustices. But real people, in real life, are actually taking Jesus' challenge to forgive. They are discovering the miraculous satisfaction of release that only mercy can bring.

Anna Kei'aho wanted justice after her son, Lopeti Kei'aho, was murdered on July 9, 2005, by a fellow Tongan immigrant, Sione Maafu Kauvaka. As the murder trial approached, she could think of little else but the relief that would come from knowing that the murderer would pay the price for such senseless violence.

But Kauvaka, instead of facing trial, pleaded guilty to the crime. He then wrote a letter filled with regret for the murder of Lopeti Kei'aho and the pain it had caused so many people. On the day of his sentencing, he intended to read the letter aloud, but ended up passing it to his lawyer. Kauvaka was afraid he could not get through it without breaking down.

Then, as a stunned courtroom looked on, Anna Kei'aho asked to address the court. She tearfully announced that she had forgiven the killer. Overcome with emotion, she had to pause to regain her composure, but her message was clear: "I forgive Sione Kauvaka."

Kauvaka received a mandatory sentence of five years to life for first-degree murder. After the hearing, the two families wept together in the hallway outside the courtroom. "Forgiveness is a big thing," Anna Kei'aho said.[20] And it's a release far sweeter than revenge.

Others are finding that forgiveness is a viable strategy. Stories recorded on www.dailyconfession.com and www.theforgivenessproject.com show the practical power of this approach.

But forgiveness on God's part is a very intricate and complicated process. It requires God to walk a very fine line between justice and mercy, in a way that only God can balance.

When we pray for justice and ask God to even the score against someone, he responds by first asking us to forgive the person ourselves; he asks us to relinquish our judicial right to retaliate. We may still hold great anger against the offender. And because God hates injustice, he, too, must be angry along with us. But when we extend mercy in God's name, Paul says that we leave room for God's wrath.[21] We're trusting him to sort things out in good time.

And it may take good time, perhaps all the way to eternity. After all, God can't even the score in a way that will bring injustice to anyone involved. If God strikes down a man who takes the life of another, could that immediate act of retaliation be unfair to that man's son or daughter? God must take all things into consideration. And he does.

For God, the end never justifies the means. He must sort

out the tangled fishing line of the entire history of humanity without cutting the line. To bring about justice for one, he can't rob freedom from another. God may wait until the end of time to sort right from wrong. It will happen, but not instantly.

In the meantime, he asks us to trust him and to know him as an intimate friend. If we will, he shares his own power and strength to love those who are not lovable. This is perhaps his truest and most surprising answer to the justice prayer—God lets us taste his mercies by giving them away.

GOD ANSWERS PRAYERS FOR JUSTICE

Sometimes our perceived injustices are entirely selfish.

> "That promotion should be mine. I worked hard for it."
> "He always forgets my birthday, so I'll just buy myself a little something."
> "If she were a better teacher, I wouldn't have had to cheat on the test."

Perhaps the answer to these prayers is that God doesn't give us the justice we think we deserve; he gives us *his* justice—tempered with mercy.

When we most grieve our losses, when we see frightening injustices in the world, and we're so angry we can hardly control our passion, perhaps God's answer is his intimate, tear-laden friendship. We're never closer to him than when we're upset by the unrighteousness we see around us and we do something about it.

It seems that the answers to our cries of injustice are as varied as the prayers we pray.

113

The existence of injustice isn't God's fault and shouldn't diminish our desire for him. Seeing injustice in the world is a reminder that we're born with a sense of righteousness that's beyond this world—it is a sense that belongs to another kingdom and should only increase our passion for fairness, for righteousness, and for justice. Then we can take those passions and redirect them toward the source of all justice.

God answers our prayers for justice. But like the elements that collide in a Yellowstone winter, there is an angry cauldron bubbling inside us waiting to spew forth emotions that can be stronger than our ability to use them for good. They can also block our ability to see his answers.

God knows this and loves us anyway.

He invites us to desire justice and righteousness so much that it moves us to action, to right wrongs, to forgive, and to passionately share the intimate pain in friendship with him—the kind of friendship that can only be experienced by two friends who have both loved and lost and yet live another day—with hope.

As our desire for justice increases, so does our desire for God.

Prayers for justice, like questioning and bargaining prayers, are the prayers God always answers.

6
CHAPTER 11
Desperate Prayers

FOR MOST PEOPLE, March 25, 2005, was Good Friday. It was anything but good for Jerry Donald and his family. A claims manager for a large insurance company, Jerry had spent the morning working in a branch office. He planned to eat lunch at home with his wife, Darlene, and their daughter, Cindy, who had the afternoon off from classes at a local college. The day was warm and sunny, a mere suggestion of the hot Atlanta summer yet to come. Jerry was on autopilot as he turned into his driveway.

"I wasn't looking where I was going and felt a large bump," Jerry told a reporter for the *Atlanta Journal-Constitution*. "I had no idea what it was I had hit. I thought maybe it was a bucket. I backed up, stuck my head out the door, and that's when I saw Cindy. She was lying there, yelling, 'I can't feel anything!'"

Cindy, a former cheerleader, had gotten a new bathing

suit and was lying in the driveway catching some early spring rays. The bump Jerry felt coming up the driveway was his daughter's head.

Jerry immediately called 911. "I stayed on the phone asking them to pray with me . . . and I just stayed in the driveway, praying and waiting."[1]

Lynne, the Donalds' neighbor, came out of the house to go grocery shopping. When she opened the car door to throw her purse in, she saw something terribly wrong next door.

She remembers the sick feeling of the scene. "Darlene was kneeling on the lawn, wringing her hands, and sobbing hysterically. Sometimes I still wake up in the middle of the night thinking about her in the grass, rubbing her knees, and saying, 'Oh, Jesus, don't let my baby die. Oh, Jesus, don't let my baby die. Oh, God in heaven, please don't let Cindy die.'"

Two parents pleading in prayer for the life of their only daughter.

A helpless neighbor looks on.

What could be more desperate?

The Last Days is an award-winning documentary about four Holocaust survivors, including Irene Zisblatt, originally from Polena, Hungary, but now living in the United States. In the documentary, Irene is talking to the camera when she becomes visibly shaken and cries as she describes the evil she experienced at the hands of the Nazis. They took away her home, her family, her life, and her dignity.

While at Auschwitz, Irene was forced to undergo inhumane medical testing. Drops were put in her eyes in an effort to change her eye color, and she was left alone in a dark cell without food, water, or light. Though she was just a child herself, it wasn't the injustices she felt that upset her the most; it was the injustices she watched other children experience. Though her eyes weren't scarred by the drops, her soul was scarred by what she saw.

> I saw trucks coming . . . and heard screams in the trucks. I saw two children fall out of a truck. The truck stopped . . . and one SS man came out from the front. . . . He picked up the children . . . and he banged them against the truck and the blood came running down. And he threw them into the truck. . . . And that's when I stopped talking to God.[2]

Irene's faith was bankrupt.

Beyond Our Control

We live in a dangerous world. Bad things happen. Evil things happen. Careless things happen. Consider these ominous realities:

- If you sneeze too hard, you can fracture a rib. If you try to suppress a sneeze, you can rupture a blood vessel in your head or neck and die.[3]
- Nearly one-third of all bottled drinking water purchased in the United States is contaminated with bacteria.[4]
- For every cockroach spotted in a kitchen, at least one hundred more are hiding in cupboards.[5]
- Ninety percent of the population age sixty-five or older are infested with eyebrow mites.[6]

- It is estimated that twenty million drivers in the United States would fail "behind the wheel" driving tests.[7]
- A child can drown in as little as two inches of water and in less time than it takes to answer the telephone.[8]

Life can turn ugly in a hurry.

Compared to the rest of the world, we live in a safe cocoon. Yet we lock our doors, secure our passwords and personal identification numbers, wash our hands, vaccinate our pets, diversify our retirement funds, and strap global-positioning devices on our children.

Even then, we live in fear.

Nothing is safe—not our churches, our high schools, our colleges, or our offices. Life is dangerous, and we live most of our lives waiting for some other boot to fall.

It always does.

unintended consequences

Elaine was on her hands and knees on the kitchen floor, playing with her eight-month-old son. She pretended to chase him. When he saw her coming, he'd giggle and crawl away from her as fast as his chubby knees would take him. As they played, Elaine noticed a stray Q-tip on the floor. If Joey got a hold of it, he would put it in his mouth, so she stopped the game long enough to pick it up and throw it away. But her diligence had unintended consequences.

Joey interpreted her quick moves as part of the game and scrambled to get away from her. In his haste, his unsteady arms gave out, his chin hit the floor, and blood gushed from his jaw. An innocent game of chase became a race to the emergency room.

The doctor's examination revealed that Joey had avoided a serious injury by millimeters. In addition to the cut under his chin, his new teeth had nearly severed his tongue. After stitches and a prescription for a bland diet while the tongue healed, they were sent home.

How does a child go from the safety and love of his mother's arms to a straitjacket tying him to a hospital bed?

"I was right there. I just wanted to throw the Q-tip away so he wouldn't put it in his mouth or choke on it," said Elaine. The thing she did to protect him was what hurt him.

Many of our actions have unintended consequences. In 1928, Alexander Fleming accidentally discovered that a blue mold called penicillium killed bacterial staphylococcus cells. His pioneering research in antibiotics has been credited with saving the lives of millions of people around the world. But the discovery of penicillin and other antibiotics has generated an unanticipated result: the bacteria have fought back, mutating to defend themselves. Over the last fifty years, many infectious strains of bacteria have grown immune to antibiotics. Superstrains of diseases considered conquered, such as tuberculosis, are rising again. Developing new antibiotics is expensive and time-consuming, and in some cases bacteria are growing resistant faster than scientists can develop a remedy.[9]

In the 1990s, genetic engineers spliced together a super-productive variety of corn called StarLink. It gained FDA approval in the United States for crops intended for animal feed, but not for those intended for human consumption.

But in 2000, StarLink corn began showing up in corn tortillas. How? In the words of Bob Dylan, "the answer, my friend, is blowing in the wind." Literally.

It seems that when one farmer planted StarLink on his forty acres, the bees, butterflies, and a west wind carried the pollen from his field into the one next to his or the one across the highway. Those fields contained crops intended for human consumption. The resulting hybrid was a genetically altered species that is now loose in the world.[10]

Other examples of the Law of Unintended Consequences:

- Rabbits were introduced in Australia for sport. But without natural predators, their population exploded. Rabbits are now a major pest across the continent.[11]
- Between 1919 and 1933, prohibition laws in the United States were intended to suppress the alcohol trade. As a result, small-time, law-abiding producers were driven out of business, and organized crime grew to fill the unquenchable demand for liquor.[12]
- Attempts by the United States government to reduce housing costs in cities through the use of rent control have discouraged landlords from developing and maintaining their properties. The result is a shortage of affordable housing and an increase in rental costs.[13]

Moral?

The world is muddled.

And there is nothing we can do about it.

Edward A. Murphy Jr., a development engineer who worked on human acceleration experiments carried out by the United States Air Force in 1949, coined an adage now bantered around water coolers all across Western civilization: "If anything can go wrong, it will." Murphy's Law, as it is called, states that actions aimed in one direction, whether

Queen Elizabeth, a Protestant. Her rule was challenged by Mary Queen of Scots and her supporters in Catholic Spain. On the day of the expected attack, Elizabeth called her nation to prayer. Church bells rang out across the countryside, churches filled, and citizens prayed for deliverance.

As the Armada's grip tightened, a sudden and violent storm arose in the Atlantic. It fell with such force that it destroyed more than half the armada of 130 Spanish warships. Five thousand Spanish soldiers perished. The English, on the other hand, lost not a single ship. To commemorate their liberation, the English forged a metal with the inscription: "God blew and they were scattered."

Prayer, they believed, had changed history.

Centuries later, Winston Churchill wrote, "The defeat of the Armada comes as a miracle. For thirty years, the shadow of Spanish power had darkened the political scene. A wave of religious emotion filled men's minds."

And this historic precedent had to be on *his* mind as he kneeled in Westminster Abbey that Sunday in 1940.

On the evening of Monday, May 27, four things happened. First, a cloud cover and a thick fog settled over the English Channel and the coasts of France and Britain. Second, the wind over the water completely ceased. The sea became as calm as a lake, a respite that lasted an entire week.[15]

Third, Hitler ordered the Panzers to pull back to allow the Luftwaffe to destroy the British army. The tanks pulled back, but the fog kept the German planes grounded. Finally, under the cloak of those clouds, 850 small English boats riding on calm waters crossed the Channel and helped to rescue the soldiers. In all, 338,000 troops were saved.[16]

History, and experience, teach us to pray.

Prayers of desperation grow from the hard knocks and pragmatic experiences of real life and our common predicament: an unflinching, unavoidable mortality.

Our ambitions outpace our capacity, and the gap cannot be spanned, no matter how hard we strive. In our best times we imagine that where there's a will, there's a way. But eventually we hit our limit, and our luck runs cold. We discover that sometimes there is no way. We run out of time, stamina, and will.

And then?

We kneel down and look up.

Our unstated hope is that through prayer we will somehow regain control of everything that feels so wildly chaotic.

prayer is pragmatic

The events of September 11, 2001, and the resulting fear drove many people to their churches and to their knees. The religious community saw a big upswing in attendance and expected the religious fervor to turn into a twenty-first-century revival. But the prayers lasted only as long as the taste of fear on our lips.

Perhaps prayer merely buys us time.

While we wait for an answer from God, we delude ourselves into thinking we've regained control. This illusion reduces our stress a bit so we can think more clearly—to perhaps figure a way out of our impossible situations.

If prayer has the potential to help the pray-er, it's likely that it also has the potential to help the object of the prayer. The sick and dying welcome our prayers for their health. Perhaps more people interceding on their behalf will turn God's attention toward their healing. This, in turn, gives the patient much-needed hope and strength for recuperation.

What if prayer is not only pragmatic *from this side* of the heavenly gates, but also from *the other side*?

In Daniel Defoe's classic *Robinson Crusoe*, Crusoe takes to the sea to flee from both his family and his religion. At first, he relishes his freedom. But his good fortune fails when his ship sinks and he is stranded as a lone survivor on an island off the coast of South America. He survives on his wits and what he comes to recognize as the providence of God. God, in fact, had let him run himself into trouble so that in his desolate loneliness he could see his need for a savior. Sometimes things have to get desperate before we turn to God.

Is that what God thinks too?

Baffling as it appears, allowing us to get to desperation seems to be God's *modus operandi*. In the book of Genesis, after the great tragedy of rebellion breaks the fellowship between God and his human friends, the chasm becomes unbearable for both sides. Only then do the lost and confused humans begin to "call on the name of the Lord."

Saints and mystics have an expression for the season of desperation that comes upon those who are serious about finding truth and coming to know God. They call it "the dark night of the soul." The phrase was first penned in a poem by St. John of the Cross, a Spanish poet and Carmelite priest who lived in the sixteenth century. St. John's dark night describes the transition phase between false contentment in normal life and true fulfillment in a life dependent on God. The interim is a season of frustration, and even depression,

125

when everything that has brought security withers away. It is a time when despair grows.

This darkness hits Christians, even those who have developed strong disciplines of prayer and sacrificial service.

Suddenly, normal spiritual practices become extremely difficult.

Nothing satisfies.

God has left the building.

For some, this turmoil leads to depression and bitterness. For others, it intensifies their despair. Eventually, if it leads to true surrender, the seeker discovers a dawn of hope, surrender, and union with God.

But it is a dangerous path. God seems to pull away on purpose, as if he is allowing the chaos to create desperation. It feels like a cruel game. The Bible even hints that at times God stacks the cards and watches the game play out. It's a risky move on his part, because free will means we have a choice as to how we will respond to his absence. Or perhaps the risk is ours.

Consider the primitive song of lament passed down to us in the Bible as Psalm 60. Israel's army was in the throes of defeat, on the run, and seeking safe refuge. In the course of their flight, David pauses to put the people's bewilderment and anger into words and to appeal to God, whom they feel has unfairly deserted them, to deliver on his past promises of victory. "You have rejected us, O God, and broken our defenses. You have been angry with us; now restore us to your favor. You have shaken our land and split it open. Seal the cracks, for the land trembles."[17]

Where is God when we need him?

It is understandable how the people feel separated from

God—humanity has felt that separation for thousands of years. But wasn't Jesus supposed to bridge that gap? Wasn't that his job? God might put us in distress to drive us to prayer, but certainly not Jesus! The New Testament is filled with stories of Jesus helping. Desperate folks often brought their rash (literally and figuratively) and risky appeals to Jesus. Jesus, after all, is our divine helper.

Jesus Heals

In the book of Mark, the writer tells the story of a woman who had been hemorrhaging for twelve years. Despite spending all she had on doctors, she found no relief. According to Jewish law, this woman's sickness made her unclean and untouchable. She was cut off from all relationships, human and divine.

Then Jesus came to her village. As the crowds pressed around him, the woman, too, pressed toward him. She told herself, "If I can just touch his robe, I will be healed."[18] On her knees and daring everything, she reached out her hand as he walked past. And she touched him.

A woman touching a rabbi.

An unclean woman spreading her contamination.

It was scandalous. It was reckless.

Jesus immediately stopped. "Who touched me?"

Peter laughed. "Everyone is touching you in this crowd."

But Jesus pressed the matter. "I felt the power of healing flow from me."

The woman's frantic faith draws out his healing, even apart from his conscious consent. Then Jesus sees her and rewards her faith, not only with the healing she sought, but also with an affirmation of her dangerous presumptuousness.

This isn't the only story like this. The Gospels describe another situation, with a leper who risks everything to come to Jesus.

Leprosy is a destructive and shameful disease. Today, medical science has the cure, but in Jesus' day, leprosy was a curse of unspeakable pain. Those with the infection suffered not only from the disease itself—maggot infestation and the stench of rotting flesh—but also from utter and complete rejection in society. For the health of the community, Old Testament law dictated that lepers live outside of the city at a safe distance. For a leper to come near a clean person was a crime punishable by death. To avoid this, lepers were obligated to yell, "Unclean!" as a warning whenever they came near another person.

But this leper comes directly to Jesus and kneels before him. The act itself is sedition. He yells no warning. He gives Jesus no opportunity to avoid contact. Instead he comes close to Jesus' feet and pleads, "If you are willing, you can make me clean."[19]

If . . .

If . . . you are willing to touch me,
and to be heir of my contamination,
to be vile and rank with me,
you can make me clean.

It is an audacious presumption. To touch someone who is unclean is to become unclean yourself. But the leper's faith is audacious. And what is Jesus' reaction? Does he back away to save himself from this man's contamination?

No.

Jesus is moved emotionally.

Moved by the man's desperation.

The man has burned his bridges. If this doesn't work, he has no other options. He might even be stoned to death. Were he playing poker, he'd be all in, every chip shoved to the center of the table.

Mark describes what Jesus did: "Filled with compassion, Jesus reached out his hand and touched the man. 'I am willing,' he said. 'Be clean!'"[20]

Jesus responded.

He reached out his hand, the very hand of God, and touched this unclean soul. And in that touch, he exchanged destinies with the contamination. The leper received Jesus' life and freedom and purity. And Jesus received the leper's pain, rot, and filth. For the same hand that touched the leper would three years later be pierced with a nail. The man's leprosy, our sin, pierced Jesus' perfect hand.

Yes, perhaps an ominous God would allow us to fall into desperate circumstances, but Jesus wouldn't.

Well, probably not . . .

But there was that one time . . .

Jesus Heals *NOT*

In the Gospel of John, there is a disturbing story about how Jesus treated a friend, a close friend named Lazarus. Jesus must have had countless meals and probably even more than a few overnighters at Lazarus's house. Lazarus was the ever-ready host to Jesus and his ragtag band of followers, so it's a big surprise when everyone learns that Lazarus has become gravely ill.

But who's worried?

Jesus is Lazarus's friend.

Lazarus and his sisters, Mary and Martha, know of Jesus'

miraculous healings; they've heard the stories and maybe even witnessed a few. So they do what anyone would do when they're sick and they're good friends with a medical professional—they call him in the middle of the night. In this ancient culture, that meant they sent a messenger to get Jesus. He was staying a few villages over. Their plan, like ours, was to get the healer to help when they needed him most.

But instead of rushing to Bethany to help his friend, Jesus does something surprising—he stays right where he is.

For two more days!

His dying friend is calling, and Jesus doesn't pick up the phone.

He lets the machine get it.

Basically, his message is this: "I'm away for the weekend; call me on Monday during office hours."

With his sisters weeping over his sick body, Lazarus takes his last breath without any help from the one who could have saved him.

A couple of days later, when Jesus finally picks up his duffel bag and starts to shuffle off in the direction of Lazarus's house, the Bible says that not only is Lazarus dead, but Jesus is glad he wasn't there before his friend died.[21]

The disciples had to be looking at each other and thinking, *Are you kidding me? Lazarus was your friend!* And like all of us, they had to be wondering, *We're your friends too. Would you allow this to happen to us?*

By the time Jesus arrives, Lazarus has been buried for four days.

When they hear the commotion coming down the road,

the sisters are angry. Mary is so mad she won't leave the house, but Martha goes to meet Jesus. "If you had been here, my brother would not have died," she accuses him.

She knows Jesus had the power to heal. She had seen him do it before. But instead of coming when she and Mary needed him most, he had deliberately stayed away. Now, Lazarus wasn't sick—he was dead.

Too late.

Don't we all feel this way sometimes?

We pray a desperate prayer, and when nothing happens, we go *emo*—the slang term teens use to describe depression and being brokenhearted. We think God has forgotten us, Jesus didn't hear our cry—or, when we're really dramatic, we think, *There is no God.*

Then . . .

if we're honest . . .

it's not that we believe any of those things,

it's just that,

well . . .

we're mad.

We're as hot as Lazarus's sisters. Like Mary and Martha, we know that Jesus has the power to intercede and change things. When we don't get our way, frankly, it makes us angry enough to curse God. If only we weren't too afraid that he might curse us in return.

When Jesus saw the women grieving for their lost brother (and angry at him for stalling), he was moved. John records the moment with two potent words: "Jesus wept."

We don't know whether he was crying for the loss of his friend or the loss of the sisters' faith in him.

Perhaps both.

He knew their pain and their hopelessness, and he felt that.

He also felt their lack of faith.

But Jesus knew the game wasn't over—he had one move left. By letting the situation grow from critical to impossible, Jesus created an even graver situation. The man's body was rotting in the heat of the earth. What could be more hopeless? At that desperate moment, Jesus spoke three words that changed the lives of everyone present:

"Lazarus, come out!"

And he did.

Perhaps Jesus allowed things to get beyond hope so his glory would be even more magnificent. While Mary and Martha dealt with the excruciating pain of their grief, they also were afraid. In their culture, women left alone without a man to take care of them had serious future concerns. But the result of their emotional ordeal had to be an unshakable faith in Jesus.

Was the price of their pain worth the gift of their faith?

GOD aND EVIL

Irene Zisblatt, the woman who gave up talking to God after seeing children tortured at Auschwitz, survived the camp and later told about it. "Liberation was like a present from the world," she said, "and that's the first time I acknowledged God again, that he is around and that he helped me to get to this point."[22]

"I don't think that God created the Holocaust," says Renee Firestone, another survivor featured in the same documentary. "I think that God gave us a mind and a heart and free will. And it is up to Man what he is going to do with his life. And I blame Man, not God."[23]

Tom Lantos, also a survivor, says, "I cannot rationally explain, emotionally explain, intellectually explain, the Holocaust. I cannot, I cannot find a place for a higher authority in this nightmare."[24] Tom has spent twenty-seven years in the U.S. House of Representatives, and he has focused much of his energy on human rights issues. The evil that was perpetrated against him became the motivation for stopping it against others.

Does God cause evil?

No. God doesn't cause it.

Once it happens, is God helpless to do anything about it?

No. He can use anything for good and for his glory. Tom Lantos may not think so, but his actions and his legislation prove otherwise.

Karen and Annette had been friends since junior high. Though they had both grown up, gotten married, and moved away from their hometown, they still kept in touch. Karen started noticing things about her husband that didn't seem quite right. His actions didn't add up. He'd say he was in one place, but friends said they saw him elsewhere. Karen increasingly caught him in lies, big and small. Eventually, a coworker witnessed what Karen suspected—Eric was having an affair.

Both committed Christians, Karen and Annette spent hours on the phone talking about love, forgiveness, and God's plan for Karen's future. Annette recalls that period in Karen's life as one of intense spiritual growth—not for Karen—but for herself. "I didn't know what to tell her," said Annette. "I found myself having to read my

Bible and pray constantly for fear I would say something wrong."

Could it be that God used Karen's painful marriage as a way to help *Annette* grow closer to him?

Absolutely.

Annette was driven to her knees in a desperate attempt to help her friend, and clearly it is the desperate who get God's attention. But that doesn't mean that God in any way condoned, endorsed, created, or encouraged the pain that Karen's husband caused. God felt Karen's pain right along with her. The adultery in her marriage wasn't caused by God; it was caused by her husband. But every time we make a move, God is able to reset the chess pieces, like a master chess player, to make countermoves that always result in a greater good.

Karen would agree.

Though she mourned the loss of her marriage and struggled to keep it together, she and Eric eventually divorced. Later, she married a man who treats her with love and respect. Now she has a beautiful son and a family that was impossible to imagine with her first husband.

Joy comes in the morning.

Perhaps it also comes in the mourning.

We believe that God doesn't *cause* bad things to happen. He *allows* us to have free will, and because of our bad choices—yours, mine, theirs, and ours—bad things happen. Humans have the capacity to do evil. And we do.

The real question seems to be, Does God allow evil to back us into a desperate corner as a pragmatic way to teach us the end of ourselves and the beginning of him?

The examples above seem to suggest so.

Others would disagree.

What is clear, though, is that God answers desperate prayers.

FULL, PARTIAL, OR NOT AT ALL?

Shayna Richardson was excited on October 9, 2005. She had started skydiving two months earlier when she turned twenty. This was her tenth dive, and this one was special. It was her first solo dive.

To commemorate the big event, she bought a new parachute and asked her instructor to dive alongside to film the jump. It couldn't have been more perfect—until she jumped.

She was falling to earth at approximately 50 mph. Around three-thousand feet, she deployed her chute. But instead of the familiar *thump* of a deploying parachute, she heard the unexpected—a snap. She found herself spinning, and she didn't know why or what to do.

She cut her primary chute in an effort to allow her reserve to deploy, but the reserve failed as well. Meanwhile, her instructor's camera caught every moment of her descent. Spinning wildly out of control, Shayna was headed straight for an asphalt parking lot.

"Right before I hit," Shayna told CBS News, "I let go and I just, I told God, I said, 'All right, I know I'm going home now. Just please don't make it hurt.' I had rationalized with myself that this was it, I was gonna die, and there wasn't anything I could do about it. So I just needed to have one last talk with God before I did."[25]

The video shows Shayna falling all the way to the ground, where she hit the pavement face first.

"Really, the last thing I remember was talking to God,"

she said. "I said, like I said, 'I'm going home. Just don't make it hurt.' And then I don't remember anything until I was in the ambulance."[26] Though she had two fractures in her pelvis, a broken right fibula, and numerous operations to put fifteen plates in her face, Shayna didn't feel the impact. God answered her prayers.

Though it wasn't her spoken prayer, Shayna's life was spared. So was another one. At the hospital, Shayna learned she was two weeks pregnant. In June 2006, she gave birth to a healthy seven pound, thirteen ounce baby boy she named Richard.

Sometimes our prayers bring tangible miracles and are answered completely. Like the case of Shayna, sometimes they are answered over and above even our deepest desires.

Or our deepest faith.

Jeff and Kathryn Johnson and their three daughters are living the American Dream. He's a successful businessman in Minneapolis. She divides her days between a career as an interior designer and her role as a mom. Their girls are smart, popular, and beautiful. Who could ask for more?

Late one winter night, a car loaded with teenagers slipped on an icy stretch of road a few blocks from the Johnsons' home and rolled into a lake. Abbey, their seventeen-year-old daughter, was in that car. Abbey broke a bone in her neck, damaging her spinal cord. After two weeks in intensive care, under the watch of some of the top neurologists in the nation, the prognosis was grim: Abbey was and would remain paralyzed from the shoulders down. Helpless and angry, the Johnsons turned to the only choice they had left—they called on God for help.

Immediately following the accident, their church

asked hundreds to pray for Abbey's life. That prayer was answered. Now there loomed a more protracted urgency: Abbey needed a new nervous system.

The Johnsons and their friends began a second vigil. From beside Abbey's bed, and from a distance, they petitioned God to extend his hand beyond the reach of the doctors' skills and restore the damaged cells in her neck. Kathryn grilled the doctors for the specific physiology of the injury. With this detail, she asked that they focus their prayers on Abbey's particular needs. Weeks passed. Abbey continued her physical therapy. Kathryn continued a tireless assault in prayer, a kind of tedious spiritual therapy.

Almost microscopically at first, Abbey's condition improved. Little by little, she regained small movements, muscle control, and nerve sensation. Everyone, including the doctors, was surprised. The following months brought advances and some disappointing setbacks. But one year later, in her college dorm room, Abbey was doing awkward, but recognizable jumping jacks. She could walk, but her gait was altered.

Sometimes our prayers are answered partially.

But sometimes—and this is the most troubling—they don't appear to be answered at all.

Jennifer recalls her first trip to Disney World with her husband and son Jordan. Jordan was two, and she was twenty-seven, but their excitement was equal. For first-time visitors, it truly is the Magic Kingdom. Everything had been done to make Jordan's visit perfect. The grandparents had footed the bill, and Dad had read all the guidebooks and knew insider tips to maximize their time on the rides while minimizing time in line.

But there was one thing that money and information couldn't control—the color of car that randomly showed up for the ride at the Tomorrowland Speedway. To a two-year-old, riding in a small car and maybe even helping to steer was the kind of fantasy that only Disney could make happen. Jordan wanted that fantasy in red. As they stood in the long line, and Jennifer held Jordan in her tired arms, he repeated his request, "I want a whed caw, Mommy. Can I please have a whed caw?"

A red car.

The Holy Grail of the Tomorrowland Speedway.

For the forty-two minutes they stood in line, Jordan remained patient, except for that one request. Now their turn was coming. There was no way to guarantee a red car. Jennifer scanned the crowd ahead and analyzed the cars on the track. It was possible, but it was out of her control.

"Jordan, let's pray and ask God to give us a red car. God says in the Bible that we can pray and ask him for anything, so let's pray and ask for a red car."

Jordan knew all about prayer; it was a frequent activity in his house. He bowed his head and clenched his chubby fists together and asked God for a "whed caw."

It was almost their turn. Jennifer looked behind them at the riders departing, and she saw it—the red car, right behind the blue one. She quickly calculated the people in front of them, and yes, it looked as if they would have the red car. God answered their prayer!

The blue car moved forward, and the older couple in front of them shuffled off toward it. Jennifer pointed to the riders exiting the red car and said, "Jordan, there is our car!"

Excitement showed in his eyes.

Until he caught the look on his mother's face.

"What's wrong, Mommy?"

Jennifer watched in disbelief as the couple in front of them split up. The old lady climbed into the blue car, and the old man waved her off. He stood waiting for the red car, and when it stopped, he climbed in. He took the red car that God had sent for Jordan.

A yellow one followed, and Jennifer instructed her husband to take it, hoping the next one would be red. It wasn't. It was blue.

The next one was yellow. She let the couple behind them go. Jordan started to get impatient. More cars passed—none of them red—and Jordan began to cry, "Mommy, let's go!" Knowing she had to take the next one, Jennifer again prayed in faith for a red car.

A green one showed up. They got in.

As they plodded around the track, Jordan yelled to his dad several cars ahead of them, he waved to his grandparents watching in the stands, and he pretended to steer the car as it bumped along the metal track.

Jennifer was so hot she could have powered the car herself. "Why? Why couldn't you make a red car appear next?" she asked God. "Was that so hard for you? Why would you promise anything, *anything*, and then not be able to come through on a red car for a two-year-old?"

Jennifer admits that it wasn't a significant prayer. Many people can't afford to eat, let alone go to Disney World on an all-expense-paid vacation. It was trivial and stupid and selfish, and in the larger understanding of the world, it didn't change the life of anyone involved. In the end, even Jordan didn't complain. He was happy to be in a car.

But Jennifer knew.

She had banked on God's promise to answer her prayer, to answer Jordan's prayer. And she knew as sure as she had circled the track in the green car—God hadn't.

Troubling, isn't it?

Maybe it's not a prayer for a red car at Disney World, but we all have prayers like that. Prayers prayed in faith and earnestness.

Prayers meant to create faith in others that end up making fools of us.

Prayer for a life to be spared that isn't.

Prayer for a marriage to be healed—it's not.

Prayer for healing—it doesn't happen.

Or does it?

Remember the story of Lazarus? Mary and Martha prayed for a healing that never occurred.

Could it be that, like Jesus' plan to raise Lazarus from the dead, there is more to the car story than we can see? A prayer that appears to be so obviously ignored is granted in some way that we can't see here and now?

To Jennifer, praying for a red car was more than praying for a car. When she invited Jordan to pray, it was a practical way of teaching him about God's promises. Her intention was to use the situation as a teaching opportunity about God's character and his Word. When God's character and promises didn't show up, she feared it would somehow harm Jordan's burgeoning faith, and it made her angry that God was willing to risk it.

But what if God had plans to answer the prayer in a different, perhaps more faith-building way for Jordan?

Like Walt Disney, if God were just fulfilling magical

fantasies, perhaps Jordan's faith could never grow and mature. But having to wrestle with God's promises and his character, perhaps Jordan (and his mom) would move to a deeper faith. There is some evidence for this. Jordan, now twelve, still believes in the power of prayer. And despite having ridden in a green Tomorrowland car, he still sees God's answers to his requests.

And Jennifer? Perhaps her faith grew when she realized that God is more complicated than her attempts to explain him. Or maybe she makes him more complicated, and it was her two-year-old who could accept the situation better than she did.

There are many promises about answered prayer in the Bible, but like Mary and Martha, perhaps we only count answers when they are speedy affirmatives, refusing any answer outside of an immediate yes.

Mary and Martha's specific prayer for Lazarus's healing went unanswered.

He wasn't cured of his sickness.

But he was raised from the dead.

After experiencing heaven and being brought back, one would have to wonder whether Lazarus's own prayer was answered.

Shayna prayed that her death would be pain free— instead she was given life. Times two.

Jeff and Kathryn first prayed for Abbey's life, which they got. Then they went back to the well for more—which they mostly got.

Perhaps Jordan did get his red car of faith, and it's only his mother who's still trying to steer.

God always answers desperate prayers.

We have to believe that. Not just to get the answers, but to believe that God has answered—that he has responded in some way. Even after Lazarus dies or we've circled Tomorowland in a green go-kart, faith helps us to see answers that are beyond an immediate yes. Faith helps us to find answers beyond those we're looking for.

Though the situation in the Donald family's driveway looked grim that Good Friday, their prayers were answered. Cindy was life-flighted to a nearby hospital where tests revealed a broken neck. She is now a quadriplegic, but she's alive. And though her body is confined to a bed or a wheelchair, her spirit soars. She brings an infectious enthusiasm to friends, family, and neighbors.

Jerry and Darlene's prayers have changed. On practical days, the Donalds pray for therapies and surgeries to restore partial use of Cindy's limbs. On faith-filled days, they pray for her to walk and run and have baby cheerleaders of her own. Their prayers are less desperate than the ones that started this chapter, but the Donalds are no less certain that they, too, will be answered.

Prayers for justice, questioning prayers, bargaining prayers—and yes, especially desperate prayers—are the prayers that God always answers.

If not here and now, then in a not-so-distant Tomorrowland.

7
THE PRAYER GOD DOESN'T WANT TO HEAR

DAVID BERKOWITZ WAS SENTENCED to serve consecutive life-term sentences for killing six people and wounding numerous others in New York City. Better known by his media-given name, "Son of Sam," Berkowitz terrorized New Yorkers for months until his capture in August 1977.

When the police caught him, he simply said, "What took you so long?"

Seeing an opportunity to save himself, Berkowitz confessed to the crimes to avoid the death penalty. He began his time in the Attica Correctional Facility, but he was later moved to a psychiatric prison and has since been moved again. Though Berkowitz has been up for parole several times, he has consistently been denied freedom.

For many, this seems like a fitting, if not just, end to a madman's life—dying a slow death in jail haunted by his past crimes.

But that's not how the story ends.

In 1987, a fellow inmate named Rick talked to David about the saving power of Jesus Christ. He gave David a small Bible and encouraged him to read it. Reading that book changed David's life:

> One night, I was reading Psalm 34. I came upon the sixth verse, which says, "This poor man cried, and the Lord heard him, and saved him from all his troubles."
>
> It was at that moment, in 1987, that I began to pour out my heart to God. Everything seemed to hit me at once. The guilt from what I did . . . the disgust at what I had become. . . . Late that night in my cold cell, I got down on my knees and I began to cry out to Jesus Christ.
>
> I told Him that I was sick and tired of doing evil. I asked Jesus to forgive me for all my sins. I spent a good while on my knees praying to Him. When I got up it felt as if a very heavy but invisible chain that had been around me for so many years was broken. A peace flooded over me. I did not understand what was happening. But in my heart I just knew that my life, somehow, was going to be different.[1]

And he was right. Since then his life has been different. David Berkowitz, a self-proclaimed former devil worshiper and murderer, now has CDs and videos of his Christian conversion story available through such reputable organizations as Focus on the Family. Dr. James Dobson isn't the only evangelical leader to support him. Berkowitz has appeared on Dr. D. James Kennedy's TV show, *The Coral Ridge Hour*, and he has endorsements from Chuck Colson. Talk show host Larry King interviewed David in prison, and during the interview, David talked openly about his newfound faith. He even led viewers in a prayer.

Are we to believe this?

Does God?

Appearances can Deceive

"All that is gold does not glitter," muses Gandalf, the wizard in J. R. R. Tolkien's *The Lord of the Rings*.[2] He is chanting a prophecy about the return of the King of Gondor, and he is warning Frodo the Hobbit not to be fooled by appearances. But Frodo and his friends *are* fooled.

When they first meet up with Strider, the Ranger of the North, they treat him with deep suspicion. His ragged clothes and vagabond ways utterly mask his royal identity. Only in time do they come to see that Strider is actually Aragorn, the exiled heir to the throne of the great Southern Kingdom. All that is gold does not glitter.

The popular image of Jesus depicts him as a meek and mild man, with blow-dried hair and blue robes. The reality we find in the Gospels is startlingly otherwise. Jesus was a carpenter; he had gravitas and a stiff dose of machismo, enough to take on the corrupt powers of his day.

He once told a story about two men praying in a temple. One was respectable—a Pharisee—the golden religious leader of his time. The other, a sorry specimen of weakness. The Pharisee's reward for his glittering prayer was immediate, an acknowledgment from all those who overheard his pompous barrage that he was a spiritual man.

That meant a lot in that culture, as it would in some

places in our world today. The Pharisee's day in church was well spent, as far as his reputation was concerned.

The Pharisees were the moral police of their place and time. When individuals broke the laws of God, the whole nation was judged. The Pharisees' self-appointed commission was to keep people from screwing up and thereby deflect the wrath of God away from the nation as a whole. The Pharisees thus established and enforced numerous trivial standards of behavior, standards so petty that no one could actually fulfill them. Even the Pharisees failed.

This particular Pharisee stood praying in the open air, loudly thanking God that he was not such a louse as the sinful man whimpering weakly beside him. He reminded God that he fasted regularly to keep his flesh in check and to prove how committed he really was.

Jesus scorned this show of religion. It was nothing—no, worse than nothing. It certainly wasn't prayer, and God wasn't listening. Jesus reserved his hottest ire for these purveyors of piety. He warned again and again that the standard they used to judge others' behavior would be the standard God applied to them.

By contrast, the other man caved in guilt and shame. He was a scoundrel, and he knew it. No pretense. No excuses. He hung his head and whispered simply, "God, be merciful to me a sinner."[3]

Which prayer does God hear?

Which pray-er does Jesus affirm as a model of piety?

Precious things don't always glitter.

The mountains of the earth hold a billion diamonds masquerading in lumps of coal.

A Honus Wagner baseball card worth a cool $2.4 million sits buried in a shoebox in an unassuming farmhouse attic outside Findley, Ohio.

An original copy of the Declaration of Independence is likely folded over as background parchment for a picture frame, and maybe one day it, too, will be accidentally purchased at a garage sale for five bucks.

What fortunes lie under your feet, or in the seat cushions of your couch?

Valuable things hide easily in this cluttered world.

How do we separate garbage from valuable treasure?

Jailhouse Conversions

As we write this book, Paris Hilton, the heir to the Hilton Hotel fortune, who became famous for, well, uh, being famous, is behind bars. Or at least we think she is.

Ms. Hilton turned herself in to police on June 3, 2007, to serve an expected twenty-three days for DUI and various driving infractions. But four days later, she was released from jail. On June 8, a judge ordered her back to her cell. She spent several days in the medical wing of the Twin Towers Correctional Facility in Los Angeles because of health concerns (later learned to be claustrophobia) before she was returned to the Century Regional Detention Facility in Lynwood, California, on June 13.

Days before the jail doors revolved, the socialite was photographed leaving a church service publicly folding her hands and bowing her head, apparently in prayer. She was photographed carrying two books. The Web site www.tmz.com ran a photo of Hilton clutching her new reading material and added the following comments:

> Hallelujah brothers and sisters! Paris Hilton has
> cometh over to the light! Can you feel Jesus
> knockin'?! Let him in!!!
> With her jail term only two weeks away, Ms. Hilton
> is pulling out the big guns to prepare for her stint
> in the pokey, carrying the Bible and *The Power of
> Now: A Guide to Spiritual Enlightenment* as she
> left her home yesterday.
> Say good-bye to the sinner—and hello to the winner!

Even the tabloids that owe their existence to the advertising dollars and readers that Hilton's photos bring in can't help but lather on the sarcasm. While in jail, Hilton called Barbara Walters (collect) and discussed her thoughts on God and the transformation that was taking place in her life. She later booked an interview with Larry King.

Spiritual conversion is good for the soul.

It is also good for the case file.

Jailhouse conversions have become such a cliché that even Hollywood makes fun of them. In a recent episode of the television show *Boston Legal*, Betty White plays the calculating Catherine Piper. While working as a legal assistant, she meets firm client Bernard Ferrion, played by Leslie Jordan. Despite Catherine's knowledge of Bernard's two previous murders, they begin a relationship.

To help their relationship (and his defense), Catherine tries to convert him:

> **Catherine:** All I'm saying is, if you killed two people
> . . . there couldn't be a better time to turn to Jesus
> Christ, your Savior.

Bernard: Under normal circumstances I'd agree.

Catherine: But?

Bernard: I'm Jewish.

Catherine: Bernie, there has never been a Jewish serial killer.

Bernard: Son of Sam. David Berkowitz.

Catherine: He was adopted. Genetically, he's one of ours.

Bernard: Well, what are you saying?

Catherine: I'm saying that if you're out there murdering people, on some level you must want to be Christian. Would you let me take you to church?[4]

For the world, jailhouse conversions are laughable, but does God laugh too?

How does God respond to jailhouse prayers?

A Real Poseur

In their tongue-in-cheek satire, *Faking It: How to Seem Like a Better Person Without Actually Improving Yourself*, the writers of CollegeHumor.com offer simple how-to formulas anyone can leverage to fake their way to the top.

The book would be funny if it weren't so true.

Want to appear wealthier than you are? Street vendors in New York sell fake designer handbags and wallets for a fraction of the money it takes to buy the real thing. A good flea market in any major city will have the latest T-shirts and tennis shoes in brand-name knockoffs.

With the Internet, you don't even have to leave home. Let your fingers do the walking—on your keyboard. Hundreds of Web sites hock faux luxury timepieces. A replica of a

$27,000 Rolex Daytona can be had for a wimpy $189. Why pay retail when only you and your jeweler know for sure?

Need to fake out your boss?

You can watch every game of the NCAA men's basketball tournament on the office computer with Web sites that offer a "boss key." When the button is pressed, a fake spreadsheet pops up on the screen. Perfect if you expect the boss to check up on you during the game.

Entrepreneurs who work from home can seduce their phone clients with *Thriving Office*, a CD that simulates the noise of a hectic office complex. There are two tracks: "busy" and "very busy." The objective is simple: lull those on the other end of the line into accepting the illusion of true productivity. All the while, you're lounging in your slippers, doing a crossword puzzle, contentedly oblivious to your own bed head and morning breath.

You can even fake a life.

From www.mobilefaker.com, subscribers can stack their personal Web sites and cell-phone photo albums with pictures of fake girlfriends, fake pets, and fake houses, all to wow the duped masses—or at least to impress the guys at the gym.

Like the modern-day equivalent of a padded résumé, personal Web sites and social networking sites allow us to spin our own histories precisely the way we want them to be seen. As Andre Agassi quipped in his infamous Canon camera television commercial, "image is everything." And if Photoshop can doctor up that image, all the better.

We can laugh about how we're pulling one over on the guys, but our kids are laughing at us. Instead of boss keys on a basketball Web site, video games have parent keys so we can't see little junior playing slash-'em-up games or read the trail of instant messages from strangers pretending to be someone they're not.

Faking it has become a way of life. In a recent survey of more than thirty thousand college students, 61 percent admit to regularly cheating in their classes. Only 17 percent claim to feel bad about it.[5]

Steven Spielberg's 2002 film *Catch Me if You Can* tells the provocative true story of Frank Abagnale Jr.—a con man of colossal genius with nerves of platinum. As a high schooler, Frank idolized his father, a dreamer who came into nasty trouble with the IRS. When his parents separated, Frank ran off to New York, vowing to recoup his dad's losses and bring his parents back together.

Abagnale posed as a Pan Am pilot, a pediatrician, and an attorney. By the time the FBI tracked him down in France, he had passed more than $4 million in bad checks. As part of a plea deal, Abagnale agreed to become a consultant for the FBI, helping to spot other sneaks and cons.

With no need for remorse, posing can lead to bigger and better jobs.

And we're all guilty of it, at least to some degree. Jennifer may not have a *Thriving Office* CD playing at her desk, but if you call her home, it's likely you'll get her answering machine saying, "I am away from my desk. Please leave a message and I will call you back." Why? As a writer, she often does interviews, and when a subject returns the call, she wants to sound professional rather than personal. "Merry Christmas from the Schuchmanns!" is fine for Grandma, but not for business. So she poses, at least a little.

RELIGIOUS POSING

Perhaps posing is even more prevalent in religious circles. Those who regularly attend Bible studies or prayer groups have likely heard a bit of prayer posturing. Maybe you recognize these prayer group members.

> **The Prayer Gossiper:** "Lord, we lift John up to you. It appears that he and Cindy have been having problems, and, as you remember, last fall they almost divorced over his drinking. . . ."
>
> **The Bible Quoter:** "Father, as you say in your Word (insert verse here), that those who rely on your Word (insert verse here) and call upon your Word (insert verse here) will be heard by your Word (insert verse here). So now we come to you and ask for help because you say (insert verse here) that if we (insert verse here) . . ."
>
> **The Exposition Pray-er:** "God, you know I haven't been feeling well since my fall on the ice last month. And God, you know that I am doing my best to be Christ-like with my neighbor. But it is so difficult when people don't fulfill their responsibilities, like cleaning the ice off the sidewalk. God, you know I have to go to a neighborhood party today, and you know that I have to get a ride from my neighbor, and you know that my knee hurts, so you know I need your help today and you know I need your strength to act mercifully toward my neighbor who doesn't shovel her ice. . . ."

It looks, smells, and sounds like prayer. But is it? Politicians know full well the power of publicly postured prayerfulness. Every president in recent memory has sought a photo op with Billy Graham. Just being in the presence of "America's Pastor" casts a glow of purity, as if spiritual integrity were contagious. A timely visit to a black church on Martin Luther King Jr.'s birthday and a visible presence at the National Prayer Breakfast in Washington are on the list of campaign stops for every candidate who seriously pursues a national office. Prayer may be good for the soul, but it is also good for the war chest.

Even honest pilgrims struggle with the right motives for prayers. Gordon, a former minister and self-described heathen, thought that changing his prayer pattern might boost his success at work. Following the formula set forth in a little book on prayer, he daily repeated the mantra that called forth blessings and success on himself. The book came with testimonials of those who'd found this type of prayer effective.

But soon Gordon began to feel dirty. "I got tired of feeling like the world was revolving around me, so I took my name out of the prayer and began to pray someone else's name instead." Gordon felt that perhaps if he asked God to bless someone else, God would be more likely to answer the prayer.

So whose name did he insert? A woman whose direct success would indirectly and positively affect Gordon.

Like a tangled web, it's hard for most of us to sort out competing motivations in our prayers—which are real, and which do we try to convince ourselves are real?

RELIGIOUS POSTURING

By the early 1970s, the tent revival scene was waning and giving way to a new wave of entrepreneurial television

evangelists. Seeing the handwriting on the wall, barnstorm-
ing preacher Marjoe Gortner thought it would be a good
time to come clean. And he found a profitable way to do
just that.

Raised by evangelist parents, Marjoe (whose name is a
hybrid of Mary and Joseph) proved to be a child prodigy in
the business of religion. He was preaching and licensed to
perform weddings by the age of four. Crowds gathered to
hear his remarkable wisdom and witness his supernatural
power to heal and prophesy the words of God. Over the
years, the Gortner family hustled millions of dollars,
moving from town to town across the Bible Belt and the
West.

Their formula was simple: preach the gospel and pass
the hat.

But in his early adulthood, Marjoe grew cynical and
tired of the act. He decided to expose what he considered a
ludicrous racket. Marjoe became the magician who would
reveal all the illusionist's tricks. His objective was to ruin
the bit and profit for every other spiritual con artist and
purge his conscience in the process.

He sold his story to a documentary film crew who followed him on his final tent revival tour. Marjoe delivered
what he promised. On film, he exposed all the tricks of his
trade. The resulting film portrays Marjoe, and by implication
others in his same calling, as shysters of hellish proportion.
The film *Marjoe* won an Oscar in 1972 for the best documentary category.

The film crew captures behind-the-scenes footage of
Marjoe's revival meetings, where he and his team mock the
duped congregants as they count piles of tens and twenties.

Marjoe acknowledges that his miracles are staged. He demonstrates how to draw a red cross with sweat-activated ink. He tosses a smoke bomb and calls it the "glory of the Lord." His deception is deliberately revealed.[6]

Most of us don't participate in such egregious acts. In fact, we console ourselves by saying we're good people. But Christians can often be religious poseurs in one way or another.

> We tell others there is a religious right way to do things.

> We don't decide where to go to college based on factual differences between schools; we "pray about it."

> We choose one job over another not because of the likelihood of pay increases and promotion opportunities but because "we were called."

> We say that we pursue opportunities not because they looked like a good idea but because "the Lord opened a door."

Are these statements sincere or just churchspeak?

Are there times when we pray with mixed motives, hoping to be heard both by God and the in-crowd at the Bible study?

And who hasn't been tempted to "teach a lesson" while praying, by saying something a group member really needs to hear?

Public prayers prayed by a minister, by necessity, have to be different from prayers prayed in private. It isn't fair to his wife or children if he prays about personal family matters. But if his public prayers are less personal, are they also less sincere or less authentic?

Sometimes, even our most noble religious posturing can appear to have mixed motivations.

So who is the judge when it comes to sincerity?

YOU BE THE JUDGE?

He appeared to be the perfect candidate for king, this Saul, son of Kish. He was tall, strikingly handsome, strong and skilled in the necessary craft of hand-to-hand combat. Most of all, he was smooth in front of a crowd, with all the natural charisma of a world-class politician. Israel felt lucky to call him their native son. They gladly crowned him, paid him tribute and taxes, and gave him their sons and daughters as servants and soldiers.

But by chapter 13 in the Old Testament history book of 1 Samuel, Saul's gig as king was a sordid mess. Samuel, Israel's prophet laureate, announced a kind of impeachment and conviction: "Saul, your kingdom will not last," he rebuked. "The Lord has sought out a man after his own heart and appointed him leader over his people."

God had rejected Saul as king for one simple reason: he was too religious.

The Philistines, a European people who had settled on the coastland south of Israel, were rising against the Hebrews. The Philistines had thousands of soldiers, chariots, and iron weapons. They were formidable, and Israel and Saul were quaking in their sandals.

Samuel, who still held leadership in the spiritual arena, had promised Saul that he would arrive at the army encamp-

ment and pray with him before the impending battle. He
told Saul to wait for him before he did anything. After seven
days, Samuel had not arrived. The army of Israel grew restless. Soldiers began to go AWOL. Saul panicked. Instead of
waiting for Samuel, he took charge and mustered up his own
religious ceremony. He made sacrifices to God—a common
mode of prayer and worship at the time. He hoped the ceremony would placate everyone's fears and provide assurance
that God's blessing would see them through the crisis.

Just as the prayer event ended, Samuel arrived. "What
have you done?" Samuel yelled.

Saul blushed and then pleaded religion. "When I saw
the men were scattering and that you hadn't come and the
Philistines were poised to attack and I hadn't yet prayed,
I felt I had no choice."

"You have done a foolish thing," Samuel said.

Why foolish?

Because he had prayed?

No, this was foolish because Saul had used prayer as a
stopgap, as something that it wasn't—a way to leverage a
mood shift in his army. Saul had manipulated people with
thoroughly religious practices.

But God won't be made a means to even a worthy end.

"This is going to cost you," Samuel announced. "Your
kingdom is rotten at the heart. God will replace you with
a king with a heart for true prayer."[7]

The danger is that postured prayer pays real divi-
dends—but not the ones advertised. It can be handy to be
seen and heard acting pious. Sacred souls will respect
what appears sacred.

It seems that God agrees with Karl Marx on at least one

point. Religion really is the opium of the masses, and God hates religious posturing with a passion. God knows the difference between prayer that is used and prayer that is misused. The Creator of the universe doesn't take lightly being an accomplice to a scam.

That's fine for God, but are *we* ever certain about someone else's motives?

Can we ever truly distinguish a real prayer from a fake one?

Can we positively attach a selfish motive to Paris Hilton's sudden and suspicious devoutness? Or to David Berkowitz's transformation? After all, we're only spectators to another's prayer project.

A genuine prayer is never addressed to us, so how would we know the true from the trite? One line may sound like a prayer and yet not be. Another may sound like a spoof and yet be as heartfelt a prayer as ever uttered. Only God and the pray-ers know for sure. And even then the pray-ers may not know their own ulterior motives.

Maybe God cares more about motives than actions. This seems to be the gist of Jesus' teaching, and his recurring rebukes of the religious right–eous. Could it be that the road to *heaven*, rather than the road to hell, is paved with good intentions?

But though God values right motives, he insists that we don't stop there. Real prayer must have accompanying evidence.

God doesn't want to hear faux prayers for show—all action, no substance.

But he also refuses to hear prayers that are all words and no action.

God looks at motives. He also looks for actions that reflect those motives.

In Isaiah 1, God breaks out into a rampage against the religious pandering of his people. He says he doesn't want sacrifices. He wants lives to match prayers. The fasting he wants is justice. Put your words into action, he says, and feed the poor. Those are the prayers he wants to hear.

"The Lord doesn't see things the way you see them. People judge by outward appearances, but the Lord looks at the heart,"[8] said Samuel when he entered Jesse's house to identify the new king of Israel. Saul had looked like a king, but looks had been deceiving. This time, Samuel looked deeper.

Jesse gathered seven of his sons. Samuel studied each strong and handsome lad. One would become Israel's next king. But as the old seer looked into the eyes of each boy, the nudge of God said, "No. Not him."

"Do you have any more sons?" asked Samuel.

"Just the youngest, down in the meadow tending sheep."

"Go get him."

Isn't it remarkable that David wasn't there? Having the famous Samuel visit the house would have been an incredible honor for the family. In our day, it would be like missing a visit from Mother Teresa or Billy Graham because you were out walking the dog. The great religious leader of Israel had come to town, and David almost missed it.

When David finally came in the door, Samuel stood and poured oil over the boy's head. Oil was the sign of royalty. Through his actions, Samuel was saying, "He's my king. He's the one with the right heart."

So what was in David's heart? What was his motivation?

Was he some kind of saint or religious zealot?

Hardly.

For starters, David had emotional issues. He might have been bipolar. Even a cursory read of the Psalms and the history books that bear his story reveals a man of amazing courage and leadership, who exhibited wide mood swings, bordering at times on madness. Then there was his lust. The seeds of his later sin were in his heart early. As king, he would later commit adultery and murder his friend to cover it up.

Was this a man after God's own heart, as he is later described?

Yep.

But it wasn't perfection or religious discipline that qualified him for that position; it was his sincere motivation to know God and be known by him.

In Psalm 63, David writes, "O God, you are my God; I earnestly search for you. My soul thirsts for you; my whole body longs for you in this parched and weary land where there is no water."[9]

This is the peephole to David's soul. Whereas Saul leveraged religion to bolster his public demeanor, David prayed in secret on a hillside at night with no one to see him but his sheep.

His passion for God was private and heart driven.

It was real.

Jesus would one day say, "When you pray, go into your closet."

David was a closet pray-er.

Later, when David's sins are made public, his repentance is bare and complete. Psalm 51 is the journal of a transparent man. David asks God to wash and cleanse him. He asks for forgiveness and to be re-created. It's not that David was sin-free; it was that David was humble and sincere in his repentance.[10]

So Samuel isn't anointing a saint; he is anointing a future sinner. And God knows that. The writer of 1 Samuel basically says that the Spirit of God powerfully came on David and departed from Saul.[11]

Could the contrast be clearer?

One loses a kingdom, the other finds his God-given destiny.

Saul used public prayer to improve his religious posture. David worshiped alone with a harp. No audience. No applause. David was intimate with God.

It seems that God, and God alone, is qualified to judge the motivation of our prayers. God, Jesus warns, is the only one competent to sort fiction from fact. He warns against trying the case at home. This, he says, is the ultimate presumption; inferring motives from another's actions is deadly. Accusing anyone of hypocrisy is itself the ultimate form of hypocrisy.

So, who wants to be the first to judge Paris?

"I DON'T WANT TO HEAR IT"

God doesn't want to hear a prayer that isn't a prayer.

He doesn't open other people's mail. And when something sounds like intercession but really isn't, he'll turn the mislabeled letter over in his hand and sadly write across the envelope, "Return to Sender." Then he'll drop it back into the box from which it mistakenly came.

> When you pray, don't be like the hypocrites who love to pray publicly on street corners and in the

synagogues where everyone can see them. I tell you the truth, that is all the reward they will ever get. But when you pray, go away by yourself, shut the door behind you, and pray to your Father in private. Then your Father, who sees everything, will reward you.

When you pray, don't babble on and on as people of other religions do. They think their prayers are answered merely by repeating their words again and again.[12]

The main point of prayer for God, and for us, is the relationship between us and him. God wants our undivided attention when we pray.

When prayer plays a double role, God won't be had.

When our prayers are aimed at others, to impress or lecture or prognosticate, or when they are aimed at ourselves as a form of a pep talk, therapy, blame-casting, or self-justification, God feels hurt and rejected. Like the young girl who tries to flirt with another boy in an attempt to make her boyfriend jealous, God can be an innocent bystander in our attempted manipulations. But God won't participate in that kind of prayer. That's not the intimacy he's looking for.

It's not the intimacy we're looking for either.

Mike McLoughlin expressed it well in a blog entry titled "A Cry for Authentic Christian Living":

There is a great TV advertisement I saw recently by the Bank of Scotland. In the advert there are a group [of] people sitting in a restaurant discussing business over lunch. A man at the table starts to choke. Another man at the table observes the man choking and starts discussing the Heimlich maneuver while the first man continues to choke and turn blue. The second man even does a pretend demonstration of how the maneuver ought to be done. The rest of the diners look worried. Finally, another man from another table gets up and grasps the first man and does the maneuver. The piece of meat pops out of the first fellow's mouth, flies across the table and lands in the lap of a horrified female diner. The second man comments "That's just what I was saying!" In closing, you hear a voice saying, "Less talk" as the words "Make it happen!" appear on the screen.

Less talk, more action. That is my motto for life. I am tired of a pretend Christianity in a pretend world. I want to see the real thing in the real world.[13]

Isn't that what we all want—to have authentic relationships with each other and with God?

But the culture we live in causes us to turn away from trusting God. We're taught to find practical solutions, even if they're empty. We learn to apply lenses of distrust and fear, and those lenses color every part of our lives. We're fearful of being mocked, we're fearful of believing something that isn't true, and we don't trust that God is big enough to sort it all out. So we try to help by making our own judgments about people and their actions. And often we're as wrong about them as they are about us.

This skepticism isn't new.

When another Saul, an infamous killer of Christians, became a Jesus-follower and changed his name to Paul, he elicited more skepticism among believers than any modern jailhouse conversion. Early Christians witnessed Saul's strange transformation and knew the power he held to introduce people to Christ. Others knew the power he had to continue persecuting believers if this conversion were some kind of ruse. Time and distance helped sort out Paul's true convictions, but in the moment, it's safe to say that many who passed early judgment were wrong about his motives.

In *Newsweek*, in June of 2007, Mark Earley, president of Prison Fellowship, identified three things he felt indicated a genuine change of heart in prisoners who claim religion: "humility, accountability, and involvement in local faith communities over time."[14] But even with those tests, all of which Berkowitz appears to have passed, many still doubt.

The prayer God doesn't want to hear is the inauthentic prayer—the one where our prayer is more about religious posing than our posture in relationship to him.

We're quick to point out the posing in others, but we're less quick to study our own posture. Perhaps instead of pointing fingers, we need to check our own hearts and judge ourselves. Here's how Jesus put it: "Why worry about a speck in your friend's eye when you have a log in your own?"[15]

What if we didn't judge the motives of others, but instead allowed God to do it? What if rather than questioning God's ability to see truth, we instead marveled at his ability to change lives?

Charles Colson, once considered a hatchet man for the Nixon White House, understands how someone like David Berkowitz can truly be transformed:

> It's a tremendous conversion story—one every bit as dramatic as that of another murderer, Paul of Tarsus.

But whenever the news media talks about Berkowitz's changed life, it's with a cynical tone. Many reporters don't hide the fact that they think his conversion is phony, something he's putting on to improve his chances of parole.

Why so much skepticism?

The answer has to do with the way many of our elites view reality. Many of them believe in the philosophy of naturalism—the idea that nature is all there is, that there is no supernatural agent at work in the world. According to this view, miracles simply can't happen.

Of course the greatest miracle is the miracle of a genuinely changed life. So when a Satanist like Berkowitz repents and follows God, there is no natural explanation. That's why such conversion stories rankle non-believers.

Twenty-five years ago, the media couldn't believe it when the Nixon hatchet man became a repentant follower of Jesus. But Scripture affirms a God Who created the universe and everything in it—and Who therefore stands outside it. So when He intervenes— in my life, or in the life of a murderer—it is, well, miraculous.

If your friends saw the Larry King interview with Berkowitz, or watched the new movie about his life, help them understand how it came about that the Son of Sam became a child of God. And tell them, as well, about the God Who exists outside of His creation, and Who is able to do things that are truly controversial— and truly out of this world.[16]

As Colson suggests, the controversy should be less about us and more about God.

A high school thespian spent weeks rehearsing his role. One scene involved his eating dinner at a table. In an effort to streamline rehearsals, props were left in the storage room, and the actor was asked to pantomime eating.

On opening night, the young actor sat down to a fully furnished table. Dinner settings complete with real food were carefully set by the props master. When the scene started, the actor did just as he did in rehearsal—he pantomimed eating with nothing in his hand—only this time to the laughter of the audience.

Sometimes when we've been a poseur for too long, we don't know how to stop.

We go on eating fake food,
praying expected prayers,
and inviting worldly distractions
into our out-of-this-world relationship with God.
These are the prayers God doesn't want to hear.

For him, it is the motivation more than the content, something we have trouble judging—whether in the jailhouse or in God's house. God is all about our sincerity. In fact, he invites any serious prayer, even when it is audaciously self-absorbed.

8
"Verily, Verily, I Say Unto Thee: Be Ye Selfish"
Audacious Prayers

ON THE MISTY, BALMY EVENING of September 5, 1492, Christopher Columbus balanced at the edge of the world, kneeling at the border of known and unknown. He was praying in a tiny church, la Virgen de la Asunción, on the outermost Canary Island, La Gomera, just off the coast of Africa. La Gomera was, for the next six weeks at least, the most western-known point of civilized humanity.

He prayed in earnest. Columbus, if anything, was earnest. What he prayed, we can only imagine. He was, after all, a deeply complicated man.

Did he pray for the safe passage and return of his sadly outfitted little fleet, of his mongrel crew, and of himself? Likely so.

Did he pray he might somehow honor the reluctant trust of Isabella and Ferdinand of Spain, who had ventured him capital in the faint hope of acquiring wealth from the East

to raise an army and win back Palestine from the Turks?
Almost certainly.

Did he pray for wealth for himself and his family? He was
not above it.

Did he pray for pardon? His scandalous affair with the
island's seductive governess, the beautiful and vicious Bea-
triz de Bobadilla, had kept his ships in port a month longer
than necessary.

Did he seek forgiveness? One would hope.

Did he pray that he might somehow rightly bear his chris-
tened name, Christopher (Christ-bearer) and fulfill what he
felt was his destiny—to take the gospel of Christendom to
heathen ports around the world? He always said this was his
intention.

Whatever the specifics, it's fair to assume Columbus
prayed for himself and the success of his pending adventure, attempting the impossible—to discover a maritime
path to India. When he volunteered for this dangerous voyage, he made it personal. It was his mission.

Never mind that other monstrous crises brewed in the
world around him. Thousands of Jews were being violently
expelled from Spain. And the Ottoman Navy, hearing of the
Jews' plight, charged across the Mediterranean. In Rome, a
new pope—Innocent VIII—made a mockery of his assumed
name.

The threats were even cosmic. A 279-pound meteorite
careened toward a violent collision with a wheat field near
the Alsatian village of Ensisheim (in present-day France).
And by the Byzantine calendar, 1492 was the year 7000—the
expected year of the Apocalypse.

Regardless of the mounting chaos that threatened the

world, Columbus petitioned God on those matters that mattered most—to him. Who could blame him?

Aren't we all selfish, even in our prayers?

In an affluent suburb, there is a megachurch with hundreds of Sunday school classes. One class is led by a teacher who is a wealthy entrepreneur. He owns his own business and lives in an expensive home in an exclusive country-club neighborhood. Each Sunday he invites members to share prayer requests. On this particular Sunday, one couple struggling to pay their bills asks for prayer for the failing transmission on their minivan. Without a cheap fix, the husband won't have a way to get to work.

A second couple asks for prayer for a friend who had been in a car accident and miraculously survived after ten hours of surgery. He has numerous broken bones in his face, and he lost an eye. Their prayer is for comfort and healing.

Hearing a pause in the requests, the teacher speaks up with one of his own: His wife's cell phone has been missing for a couple of days. Would the class pray that it be found?

When the weekly prayer reminder is sent out later that week, class members who weren't in attendance are incredulous. How could the teacher, a man of wealth and power, a man who could replace a lost cell phone with the snap of his fingers, make a mockery of the prayer requests by asking for something so trite in the midst of so many greater needs?

Shouldn't he know better?

Consider another ill-timed request. Bob and Carrie host a monthly small-group meeting for their church. When the six couples arrive, Bob and Carrie share their good news. After months of trying, Carrie is pregnant with their second child!

169

A month later, the news isn't so good. Carrie shares with the group both the physical and emotional pain of having miscarried their much-desired child. When Carrie pauses to wipe her tears, Ryan blurts, "Suzi and I are having a baby! We could really use your prayers!"

The room grows icily quiet as everyone stares at the floor. Even Suzi is surprised. She and Ryan had agreed in the car on the way over not to tell anyone until they were sure the baby was healthy.

Carrie breaks the silence with her sobs. She gets up and runs to her bedroom. Bob follows.

Doesn't Ryan know that it is out of place to ask for such a thing when God obviously denied it to someone else?

We have a sense of moral righteousness about the prayers that ought to be prayed, those that ought not be prayed, and even the right time to pray certain prayers. The Bible teaches that we can pray about anything, but church members frown on prayers that seem self-seeking and greedy.

Yes, we're all guilty of praying selfish prayers. And yet it seems that God sometimes even answers them. How can this be?

selfish prayers

Our own personal Copernican Revolution occurred at an inconspicuous moment between our fourth and seventh months of life. Just as Copernicus discovered that the earth isn't the center of the solar system, we discover we aren't the center of the world. We are playing with our toes, pulling the dog's tail, or refusing to eat, when for the first time we recognize that Mommy is not present. Worse, we

grasp the terrible truth that we have no control over making her reappear. Even with our most full-throttled scream,
it takes seventeen eternal seconds for her to run in and
swoop us up.

In those seventeen seconds, we begin to see ourselves
as separate; we are our own person, and alone in the world.
It is a terrifying and strangely wonderful moment. After
that, our lives become a series of fragmented moments that
either reinforce or dispel our centric view of ourselves and
the world around us.

While speaking at the Catalyst conference in October
2006, Donald Miller, author of *Blue Like Jazz*, talked about
the feeling of being at the center of our own world. He
describes it this way:

> My life is a movie, and the movie is about me. And I
> can prove it; if I leave the room—I go with me. I have
> two cameras and a microphone, and I have been in
> every scene from the very beginning.
>   You have always thought life was a movie about
> you. [But] you are character actors in a movie—about
> me. It isn't a very interesting movie, yet the data sug-
> gest that it's true.[1]

At times, we all believe we're the star of our own show,
the leading actor in our own drama, or the diva of our own
opera. By default, everyone else must be bit players—the
point of their lives is to make our star shine brighter. At
other times, we recognize we have no control, and we
seek those who do—parents, teachers, or Supreme Court
Justices. The phenomenon of prayer reflects this strange,

universal tension. We want to do it our way, yet we simultaneously seek an insider's connection with the Big Guy upstairs. So we strike a balance.

We pray to God, but we pray selfish prayers.

When we pray, we mostly talk about ourselves, on behalf of ourselves, to bless ourselves. It's our way to have cake and consume the crumbs too; to run wild with the credit card and let Father pay the bill.

Intentional or accidental, we're all guilty of selfish prayers.

"Lord, please don't let my baby die."

Sometimes we defend them as righteous.

"Lord, please destroy all the terrorists."

At other times, we don't defend them at all.

"Lord, please let me win the lottery. I'd sure look good driving a red Corvette."

Nowhere are me-centered prayers more confusing than at a sporting event. Yankees fans pray to slaughter the Red Sox; the Red Sox pray to wipe out the Yankees. (Without injuries to either team, of course—after all, it's a prayer.) Is God a Yankees or Red Sox fan? Answering one selfish prayer certainly leaves another unanswered.

Sometimes our prayers are desperate cries for things we really want.

"Lord, please bring him home; I promise I'll be a better wife."

But we also pray for things we're not sure we want.

"God, please help me stop smoking."

We get so focused on ourselves that our prayers can actually keep us up at night. Bill Cosby once joked, "Now I lay me down to sleep, I pray the Lord my soul to keep. If

I should die before I wake . . . oh no, I'm not going to sleep tonight!"

Prayer under Fire

A soldier hit by a limb-tearing bullet cries, "Why me?" His combat buddy, who returns home safe and healthy, prays, "Why me?" In each case, the soldier believes that he doesn't deserve the situation he is in. There is an underlying assumption that circumstances could be different, that we're owed better, or at least owed an explanation for why we're in this situation. Our most selfish prayers are predictable. They express a desire for something better and an understanding that the answer comes from God.

In an episode of *The Simpsons*, Bart is faced with the possibility of flunking fourth grade. To be promoted, he must pass a test he hasn't studied for. He prays to God, asking for more time:

> Well, old-timer, I guess this is the end of the road. I know I haven't always been a good kid, but, if I have to go to school tomorrow, I'll fail the test and be held back. I just need one more day to study, Lord. I need Your help! A teachers' strike, a power failure, a blizzard. Anything that'll cancel school tomorrow. I know it's asking a lot, but if anyone can do it, You can. Thanking You in advance, Your pal, Bart Simpson.[2]

Bart's prayers are answered when, overnight, a snowstorm arrives and school is canceled. His sister, Lisa, acknowledges the connection:

I heard you last night, Bart. You prayed for this. Now your prayers have been answered. I'm no theologian. I don't know who or what God is exactly. All I know is He's a force more powerful than Mom and Dad put together and you owe Him big.[3]

This example is just a television show, but we've all experienced something similar—a time when we prayed for something totally selfish and received the answer we were hoping for. Answers to our prayers keep us coming back to ask for more. We understand there is something better— whether we believe it is temporal or eternal—and somehow we recognize that God is related to that. So we send up both noble and perverse prayers, and we count on God to sort them out. Surprisingly, he listens to selfish prayers.

Paul, a young U.S. Marine, was stationed in Iraq during the height of President Bush's troop surge. In the years before his deployment, Paul struggled with his faith, battling to reconcile the fire and passion in his bones with the image of the mild and gentle Jesus he grew up with.

How could a wussy Jesus also be the God of the frontlines? A place where friends get their legs ripped off in roadside bombs?

Assigned to a mission that would take him away from his Iraqi base for two weeks, Paul feared what that mission might involve. The thought emboldened him. To discover how big God is and whether or not he cared about the little things, Paul began to pray for more than just safety—he began to pray for special favors.

Paul's rank—official military title of "low man on the totem pole"—meant that he often got the worst assignments. When it is 130 degrees, you don't want to be the guy forced to do vehicle maintenance outside. One such day, he decided to ask God for a favor: "Get me out of the heat today. I don't want to go out there." His assignment that day? Packing water bottles in the walk-in cooler.

Then he asked God for chicken cordon bleu to be served in the mess hall. It was.

Two days later, he asked for it again. Again, it was served.

"I'm asking for special treatment, and I expect God to listen," said Paul. He's not concerned what anyone else thinks about his prayers. If they want to ask for favors, too, they can.

The fire of battle changed his prayer life. There isn't time for flowery poetry when you fear for your life. Combat drives things to the core. If a soldier prays, it has to work. God has to be as practical as a field manual, or he's too heavy to carry into combat. Living in fear, with constant threats on his life, drove Paul to stop the religious niceties he had been brought up with. Paul gave up wussy prayer, and when he prayed selfishly, he found out God was strong enough to hold his own.

At eighteen or nineteen, Jennifer attended a prayer seminar where the leader asked everyone to pray for whatever they wanted; no request was too big or too ridiculous. Jennifer prayed some pretty presumptuous prayers for a girl her age—she wanted a house and a red car that she didn't have to pay for. She also listed five or six other, smaller items. As instructed, Jennifer wrote the prayer requests down. She prayed over them for several days, until she got busy or just forgot.

Months later, Jennifer found the list of prayer requests

in her Bible. As she looked down the list, she realized that each request she'd prayed for had been granted. She was caretaking a friend's house, living there rent-free. She'd also been given a blue car by a friend. (She couldn't help but wonder, if she had waited, whether a red car would have come along.) Smaller requests had all been fulfilled too.

Bart Simpson got his day off from school.

Ryan and Suzi, despite their ill-timed prayer request, eventually had a healthy baby boy.

The Sunday school teacher's wife found her cell phone—in a forgotten bag.

And Columbus discovered America.

God continues to give us cake—and lets us eat it. We spend and he picks up the bill.

Of the six prayers that God answers, this is perhaps the most confusing. We want to believe that God only answers selfless prayers, but the truth is he answers selfish prayers: noble, perverse, self-serving, and insensitive. He does it for good people and bad; for those who recognize his answers and those who don't; for people who have relationships with him and people who don't.

As a matter of experience, it seems that those he often rewards the most are those who ask the most.

Audacious Prayers

In the Broadway musical *Fiddler on the Roof*, Tevya, a Jewish Russian peasant, debates God in prayer while he milks his cows. "Dear God, you made many poor people. I realize, of course, that it's no shame to be poor. But it's no great honor either! So what would have been so terrible if I had a small fortune?"

176

Tevya comes to God with the candor and good humor of an intimate friend, slightly embittered by what he sees and experiences around him. He knows full well that a blessing was promised to his forefathers, and he wonders aloud, "So what about me?"

The Bible reveals many Tevya-like prayers, challenging God to live up to his word. Surprisingly, the God of the Bible doesn't seem averse to answering me-focused prayers. He actually seems to encourage them by rewarding blatant self-interest.

People in the Bible who get what they desire from God usually approach him with a good measure of chutzpah. They believe that God exists, and that he is powerful, but they also sense that they personally have some right to impose on him. They may not view themselves as equals, but they confidently approach him anyway. At first blush, these stories seem almost blasphemous. But God never seems offended.

There is an old story of a man who needs to borrow food to feed his guest. In this ancient Jewish culture, hospitality is an important virtue. The man has had an unexpected visitor in the middle of the night, and he is obliged to house and feed the guest. To have no food for a guest would be a flagrant insult. So the host goes to his friend's house and begs his friend to let him borrow some food.

The friend is unmoved. "It's too late at night," he objects.

But the host persists. Finally, the friend complies and gives him food.

As Jesus tells this story, he makes the observation that boldness and importunity, not friendship, are what eventually turn the friend's heart.[4]

The parable seems to suggest that audacity is the key to getting a response from our prayers.

Really?

Audacity?

This is contrary to our thinking that the relationship is what gets the result.

Shouldn't the friend have shared his food with the host because he was his friend, not because he kept knocking, keeping everyone awake in the middle of the night?

In another parable, Jesus tells the story of a widow who comes to a judge seeking a settlement against those who had wronged her. The judge isn't interested in hearing her case, but the widow persists until he finally offers her justice.[5]

We find repeated askers annoying, but as any parent of a toddler will attest, we often give in to them.

Doesn't God have more patience than that?

Surely he's not saying, "Just keep asking. Doesn't matter whether we're friends or not; if you ask enough I'll get tired of listening to you and just send you away with what you want."

Why would God reward persistence over relationship? Isn't relationship important to God? For God to reward persistence, there must be something else going on.

Prayer Promises

Humans are God's crowning achievement.

According to the Bible, God created humans with freedom and awareness so that he might have a real relationship with us. His risk was significant because he released control. Humans were given the opportunity to walk away with their individuality intact and ignore him. But without individual freedom in his subjects, God would be nothing more than a puppet master.

He placed instinctive obedience in every other creature, but he risked relational partnership with us. And God got burned in the gamble. We choose to walk away more than we choose to walk toward him.

Unless of course, we want something.

Maybe that's why God likes persistence—it offers him the possibility of developing a relationship.

Rather than handing over our requests the first time we knock at the heavenly gates, perhaps the relationship is so important to God that he accepts less. A connection that involves us standing at the door for weeks, knocking, ringing the bell, and occasionally kicking the door, is better than not having a relationship with us at all.

Could it be that when we withhold ourselves from God, he'll take the only relationship he can get? The one he finds in our persistence?

This characterization makes God sound like a lonely, old widow who offers a check if her son will visit, hoping the occasional contact will jump-start a more regular relationship. Like the old lady, could it be that God longs for something more?

He's not obligated to do anything for us. But the Bible repeatedly tells us of his love for us. If we take the ancient texts at their word, it seems that God gives, not out of hoping to get, but out of his love for us.

Instead of the image of a lonely widow, perhaps God is more like a doting grandfather. The cost doesn't matter. He just wants to see his grandbaby smile. Throughout the

Gospels, Jesus makes some very direct and audacious promises on behalf of his father. Frankly, he says some pretty crazy things about personal prayer.

> Whatever you ask for, believe you will receive it and it will be yours.[6]

> Ask and it will be given to you, look for it and you will find it, knock and the door will open.[7]

> Having faith in the amount of a small seed is enough to move mountains into the sea.[8]

> If you have faith, you will do things that are even greater than what Jesus did. When you speak to God, just remind him that Jesus said this, because that helps bring glory to God. Ask anything you want and he will do it.[9]

> Remember Jesus' words; live them and ask whatever you want and it will be given to you.[10]

> Have faith. Don't doubt and you will get whatever you ask for in prayer.[11]

> Ask anything in his will and he'll hear you. Whatever you ask, you have it from him.[12]

> Nothing will be impossible for you.[13]

Is God trying to tell us that if we ask big and we ask often, we're more likely to receive?

If so, why don't we all join hands, sing "Kumbaya," and pray to win the lottery?

It's confusing, isn't it?

Our mother leaves the room when we're an infant, and we quickly learn we don't always get what we want. Our first play date, or the birth of a sibling, teaches us we have to share. Yet, like a noncustodial parent at Christmas, our Father tells us to ask for anything, and then he promises a bounty bigger than we expect.

Which is it? Are we polite and careful in our requests, or bold and audacious, expecting it to rain presents from heaven?

Hardwired Selfishness

Have we ever considered that perhaps God made us selfish?

Maybe being selfish isn't a part of our sinful nature, but rather comes embedded as original hardware. This seems like a profane thing to say, something a secularist would believe. In fact, many of them do.

In classical mythology, Narcissus was the handsome mortal youth who rejected the amorous advances of the nymph Echo. Echo became so distraught over this rejection that she hid herself away until all that was left was her whisper. The goddess Nemesis heard Echo's prayers for vengeance and doomed Narcissus to fall in love with his own reflection in a pool of water. There he sat perpetually, gazing longingly at his own image until he died.

Are we not all Narcissus?

Charles Darwin called self-seeking behavior the driving force behind all life. Life, he theorized, is a battle for personal survival. With the map of the human genome complete, Darwin's speculations are—in the minds of many—all but confirmed.

The scientific consensus seems to be that humans are gratification machines. Our selfish behavior is simply and irreversibly hardwired into our code. What pushes us is a simple, uncluttered compulsion to survive and to pass on our successful genetic blueprints to another generation.

Could it be that God intended it that way?

In *The God Gene: How Faith Is Hardwired into Our Genes*, Dean Hamer argues that religion is preprogrammed into our chemistry. Hamer even claims to have identified one of the genes responsible for religiosity. Religion, he contends, is a great pacifier.

While adrenaline gave our ancestors the boost to sprint away from an attacking lion, the stress of their environment dooms them in the marathon of life. Hundreds of studies on the negative effects of stress demonstrate that relaxed creatures survive. Evolution has therefore selected humans who can manufacture calmness by fabricating belief in a god. Hamer says that feelings of spirituality are due to nothing more than a shot of intoxicating chemicals flooding our brain.

And they're there for our own good.

Achilles fought the Trojans fearlessly once he had donned his Olympian armor, because he thought it made him invincible.

Dumbo the flying elephant soared over the circus crowd as long as he held his "magic" feather, which he believed gave him power.

Prayer, according to Hamer, leads us to think we are both powerful and at peace.

Could prayer be God's armor or a magic feather for believers?

It does appear that prayer is good for our survival. Perhaps selfish prayer even more so. It calms and relaxes us. It reduces stress. And it buffers us with the belief that we have some advantage. Perhaps we do.

A scientific study of nearly four hundred heart patients found that those who were prayed for—without their knowledge—were dramatically healthier than those who received standard medical treatment alone. Patients who were not prayed for were nearly twice as likely to suffer complications—more than twice as likely to suffer heart failure, three times more likely to require diuretics and to suffer pneumonia, and nearly five times more likely to need antibiotics—as were the patients who received special prayer. The statistics were dramatic, demonstrating that there was only a 1/10,000 probability these results would happen by chance.[14] Prayer might in fact be very good medicine.

And what could be more selfish than good medicine? When we take aspirin for a headache, we take it because it has specific advantages for us right here and now. We don't say to the bottle, "Well, if it is aspirin's will to relieve my headache, then so be it."

Hardly. We impose our will on the medicine by pulling out a pill and placing it on our tongue. Swallowing the pill puts it in a place where it can work.

Why do we do this?

Because it is in our own best interest.

Could it be the same with prayer? If prayer really is good medicine, then the act of prayer itself could be considered selfish.

In the Old Testament, the word for salvation is closely connected to the word for healing. Few believers have reservations about praying for salvation—in fact, Christians often feel it is their mission to recruit nonbelievers to pray the prayer of salvation because the Bible promises eternal life for those who accept God's gift of grace.

But isn't an existence in eternal bliss the same as praying for health here and now? They are both requests for a personal favor—something out of our reach that requires God's intervention.

Perhaps God created us with unquenchable desires—desires for successful outcomes—that he knows we can't satisfy ourselves. Could it be that those desires are the very things that bring us back to him?

If so, he loaded the dice in the game of life.

He gave freedom, only to entice us back into a relationship by making our desires impossible to fulfill outside of a partnership with him. We are cowboys parading our toughness, independence, freedom, personal responsibility, and self-determination as we hum our real national anthem, "Don't Fence Me In." We want our freedom, but we also want our magic feather. No point in being stupid about it—we'll take both.

God is sly. He plants self-desire in us, desire that can never be filled. Then he coaxes us to pray, to ask him for what we cannot muster in ourselves. This is the paradox: Our most selfish prayers are our truest form of humility—a denial that we are sufficient in ourselves. Even selfish prayers demonstrate a trust that only through prayer are all things possible.

BaIT aND SWITCH

Kim and Joel Sheagren prayed for a child. Their prayers grew out of one of the deepest instinctive compulsions known to humankind: their desire to transfer themselves to another generation. These are selfish prayers, planned and planted by God.

Kim and Joel asked, but soon learned they couldn't conceive. Faced with this knowledge, they suffered the pain of not being able to fulfill their desire, while simultaneously being angry about the world around them—a world where infants are left in garbage bins, babies are born to crack abusers, and fathers shake their babies to death.

In time, Kim and Joel began to see their prayers differently. Rather than search for a baby that looked like them, they decided to look for a baby that needed them. The Sheagrens began the process of adoption.

On the day Sam was born, his birth mother sat in her hospital bed with Sam in her arms and Kim and Joel at her side. In that small room, a miracle took place in her heart. Her intuitive motherly love was gently removed just as Kim's instinctive motherly love strangely awakened. The genetic drive gave way to a deeper, purer love. An inexplicable desire was born in the Sheagrens to lay down their lives for another person's child. The outcome wasn't the one they had originally planned, but somehow it was more deeply satisfying.

This is the teaching we glean from many books on prayer. God supplants our original request for one that is better, deeper, more noble or profound.

And there is some truth to this.

What father, Jesus asks, would give a snake to a child who asks for a fish, or a scorpion to the child who asks for an egg?[15] Likewise, when our children request chocolate cake for breakfast, we give them blueberry pancakes, not as a compromise, but as wise and loving parents who see in their childish request both the desire for something sweet and the need for something healthy.

As authors of a book, perhaps instead of spending our time writing, we should be on our hands and knees praying for sales. Perhaps our first prayer should be that the book is a huge success, that it sells millions of copies and makes everyone involved rich and famous.

But somehow it feels nobler to pray a different prayer. Perhaps a prayer that we will have the focus needed to finish writing the book before the summer deadline, so we can still enjoy vacation time with friends and family.

Why aren't we as bold with the first prayer for success as we are with the second prayer for time with our family?

Frankly, the first prayer sounds selfish and self-serving. Many people see authors as celebrities, and the prayer seemingly reaffirms that view by asking for riches and fame. But if we believe what we've written, God seems to encourage prayers for selfish ambition. He rewards audacity and persistence. According to God, there is nothing wrong with that kind of prayer. But as pray-ers, we have to admit that something about that prayer doesn't feel right. A prayer for focus to finish the job and spend time with family somehow seems nobler.

Perhaps there is more to it than we see with our worldly and judgmental eyes.

Both authors give away a percentage of their incomes to charities; increased royalties means more money to fund needy organizations. Both authors volunteer their time and experience to groups that can't afford to pay them. Could their (prayed for) fame attract more volunteers to those same organizations?

What if riches and fame to the authors imparted the same fortune to their publisher or agent—who could then take risks on unknown authors who write books for smaller audiences but provide insights to larger problems?

When looked at from this perspective, could it be that asking for riches and fame is a noble prayer after all?

Likewise, a prayer for clear thinking and focus could be disguising a desire for the writing experience to be easier. Perhaps that prayer is code for "get us out of the hard work of disciplined writing and on to something fun."

There are other prayers that could be prayed. That the editor would like it, or that readers would be helped by it. A case could be made that each of these prayers is selfish. If the editor doesn't like it, hours of rewriting will be necessary. If readers are helped by it, our sense of importance is increased.

After all, why do readers need this book? Couldn't we just pray that readers would be helped by any book? Or without a book at all?

Which prayer is the appropriate prayer?

Which prayer is God most likely to answer?

Maybe the answer is "all of them."

God sees something more in the apparent triteness of our selfish requests. Perhaps like a secret agent with a decoder ring, God reads a prayer "for a lost cell phone" as actually a prayer for a deeper need—like the need to know that God is present even in the small things.

Or maybe not. Maybe God just appreciates any kind of relationship, even if it is just a short prayer about a missing cell phone.

Perhaps a prayer for earthly riches is really a cry for eternal riches and a meaningful life.

At small group, when Ryan so insensitively blurted out the joyous news of his wife's pregnancy, did God know that he didn't mean to hurt Carrie's feelings?

Though the others in the small group didn't know it, God knew that Ryan wasn't being insensitive or self-absorbed. Rather, Ryan identified so closely with Carrie's loss that he brought his concern to the throne of the only one who could give and take life—to beg in prayer for the life developing inside his own wife's womb.

The most selfish prayer prayed with faith and belief in God has an equal chance of being answered as the noblest prayer. God is waiting for us to speak our desires, to ask and keep asking, so that he might give and keep on giving.

He longs for us to presume on his goodness, to expect his favor. He wants to be thought of as generous, even more than he wants to be feared as just.

God hears what we say, and like a great dad, knows what we really mean. He might be Awesome Creator in relation to the galaxies flung across the heavens; he might be a valiant and vengeful King to the demons of hell; but the Bible says he is our Papa. The prayers that sound so selfish to our human ears have a different ring when they echo in his. Perhaps that is why *we're* the ones who get bent out of shape by seemingly greedy prayers.

God doesn't.

In fact, he suggests we ask for more.

THE ASK

God doesn't care as much about the outcome as he does the ask.

If we review the parable of the host borrowing food from

his friend, we see that the request wasn't made of a stranger. The request was made in the context of an existing friendship. The host didn't go to just *any* house to borrow food; he went to his *friend's* house.

What God implies is that the relationship is the basis for getting to make the ask—but it's not sufficient to receive the outcome we desire. In the case of the host, he also needed persistence. Jesus' words suggest that relationship is important, but he uses other conditions, too, like faith, belief, remembering and living out Jesus' words, using Jesus' name, and asking in agreement with God and others.

There is an implication that a relationship is already present. And within the context of that relationship, God has given us a check full of grand promises. It's up to us to cash it.

A desire for greatness is assumed.

It is the bait he uses.

The twist Jesus introduces is the *way* to greatness.

There is an irrefutable conflict here. We pray to win the lottery, and yet we don't. We ask in faith. But we don't receive.

There are well-intentioned preachers who tell us it's because we don't have enough faith—but God says it takes only a mustard seed to move a mountain into the sea. How much faith could it take to move a Powerball with our number on it into the chute?

From the time we first prayed a big, audacious prayer, and it didn't happen like we thought it would, we've had questions. We ask whether or not God's promises are true. If they are, and we didn't get what we ordered, it implies something might be wrong with him . . . or us. Maybe we didn't pray correctly, we didn't have enough faith, or per-haps it's as simple as we asked for the wrong thing.

So we learn to diminish our prayers. Instead of praying, "God, I'd really like that job at Google," we soften the blow of rejection by adding, "if it's your will." Soon, our interces-sion to the Sovereign of the universe gets bundled with a rabbit's foot, salt thrown over our shoulder, and a horseshoe over the door. We temper and change our *asks* in hopes of increasing answers that match our preferred outcomes.

But let's look at our asks a little deeper. Our asks are made up of our desires; our desires drive our asks.

Could it be that we desire much but we ask too little?

C. S. Lewis explains in *The Weight of Glory*:

> Our Lord finds our desires not too strong, but too weak. We are half-hearted creatures, fooling about with drink and sex and ambition when infinite joy is offered us, like an ignorant child who wants to go on making mud pies in a slum because he cannot imagine what is meant by the offer of a holiday at the sea. We are far too easily pleased.[16]

God plants unquenchable desires in our hearts that have no human way of being reconciled.

We pray for a boyfriend, but God offers us eternal love.

We pray for enough money to make it to the next pay-check, and he offers us a Kingdom.

Could it be that he is answering our prayers—our deepest desires—and we're refusing to accept his gifts?

The English philosopher John Stuart Mill believed that even virtues could be pleasures in disguise. He contended that all our choices are motivated by a desire to be happy. So, from Mill's perspective, even someone like Mother Teresa would have given selflessly to the poor because giving was her truest pleasure. According to Mill's point of view, it could be said that Mother Teresa was fundamentally selfish. Would she have agreed? Perhaps. She certainly seemed to have a purpose and joy that so many of us "less selfish" humans don't have.

IT'S YOURS, KID

God, it seems, is offended when we take too little thought of our own eternal self-interest. His critique of our lives has less to do with our greed than with our fear to take up, by faith, what is already rightly ours. This is Jesus' stern warning in one of the greatest stories ever uttered from human lips.

A wealthy father had two sons. The younger asks for his inheritance while the father is still living. In that society, such a request was tantamount to saying, "Father, I want you dead!"

Yet, instead of resisting or even retaliating, the father delivers half the estate to the boy, who promptly goes abroad and squanders the treasure. Eventually, the impoverished son comes to his senses and heads home again, hoping to be accepted as one of his father's servants. The father, who had been watching for his son every day, runs to meet him on the road, throws his arms around him, prepares a great feast, and brings him back into full relationship as his son and heir.

But the older son is infuriated. He complains that his father has never thrown a feast for him and his friends, though he has remained faithful to the family covenant. His father responds that everything in the estate has always been his. He could have asked for anything, at any time!

When we pray to win the lottery, what we're praying for is a more comfortable life for our family, the ability to quit our job, or to have luxuries we desire. But what if answering that prayer exactly as we pray it means that our family changes, we no longer have meaningful work, and our friends are jealous of our wealth?

A West Virginia man who won $315 million in the lottery would give it all back to have the life he had enjoyed with his wife and granddaughter before winning the big prize. After he received his payout, he spent time in jail for drinking, had hundreds of thousands of dollars stolen from his car, had his wife divorce him, and lost the granddaughter he dearly loved after she became addicted to drugs that eventually killed her.

Perhaps when we pray to win the lottery, we're corrupting the real prayer; we're playing in the sandbox when we could live at the beach.

Could it be that our prayers for cars and money are perverted prayers for our real desires of eternal treasure and heavenly streets of gold?

If so, what other kinds of longings have been corrupted? Maybe the ask isn't about us.

Maybe it's about God.

Remember Donald Miller's description of his life as a movie—starring him? Here's how he finished that story:

> No logical evidence suggests life is about me. If life is about anything, it is about us, and I would even say it's not about us so much as it is about God. Life is just

a story about God and we get to be in it. That's it. We have the pleasure of interacting with a story that he is slowly and methodically telling himself, and he is enjoying every twist and turn because he knows it's going to turn out for his glory and for our good if we trust and have relationship with him. That's the story.[17]

That's the story?

That we're just bit players?

That is the heart of George MacDonald's fantasy novel *Phantastes*. We are players but never heroes in our story. And the story we land in and live is someone else's tale. Our role is to shine our light on someone else, to make him successful and blessed. We live our selfish lives best when we fulfill our role to bring "happily ever after" to the bigger story. We're not asked to be selfish in the worldly sense, but selfish in the eternal sense—to demand nothing less than what God made us for.

God's objection to ambition is not the benefit it seeks, but the means employed to get there. Jesus bluntly tells his followers, "If you want to be great in the kingdom of heaven, be the servant of all. If you want to be first, be the slave of all."[18]

So how do we serve? How do we best fulfill our roles?

Use our talents to their fullest, especially in service to others.

Desire riches and glory beyond the trinkets this world offers.

Bring greater honor to the Storyteller than to the characters in the story.

Columbus traveled great distances to change the way we view the world. Our selfish prayers can take us on a journey with the potential to change the heavens. Bargaining and questioning prayers, prayers for justice, desperate prayers, and audacious prayers—these are the prayers God answers—if only we're bold enough to ask.

9
"please, sir, i want some more gruel"
Prayers of Beauty and Happiness

on a clear summer afternoon in 1977, Mark sat on the crowning granite boulder atop Mount Hooper in the Sierra Nevada range and looked out across the world. At 12,349 feet, Mount Hooper is far from being the tallest peak in the Sierras, and it isn't the most technically difficult to climb, but the view from the peak made those details irrelevant to Mark.

The staggering peak of Mount Whitney, the highest point in the continental United States, shaped his view of the southern horizon. To the north stood the fabled domes of Yosemite Valley, which Mark had often gazed at from the valley floor but until now had never seen eye to eye. To the east lay hundreds of miles of emptiness—the deserts of California and Nevada—looking like a vast golden sea. To the west, wrapped in a cloak of fog, stretched the immeasurable Pacific Ocean.

On that day, Mount Hooper became *his* mountain.

. . .

The door to the Galleria dell'Accademia is unimpressive. Tucked away in the narrow and crowded streets of Florence, tourists who stumble across the door turn and ask, "Where's the main entrance?" But for those who venture through the door, walk to the line at the ticket booth, and then down the exhibit hall to the rotunda, the confusing effort is worth the sight. There, at an imposing seventeen feet tall, stands Michelangelo's statue of David. The height itself is impressive, the artistry more so. Carved from a single "useless" piece of Carrara marble, the work is breathtaking.

John and his wife slowly walked around the statue and observed the bulging veins and the straining muscles of arguably the world's most recognizable piece of sculpture. But something even more impressive caught John's eye. His six-year-old son, Ricky, had staked out a piece of museum floor in front of the statue and spread out his tools, a children's travel journal with blank pages and pencils from his backpack.

Oblivious to the people stepping over him, he squatted, intently eyeing the statue. Though he had never been especially enamored of classical art, something in the beauty of the statue called forth the artist from within him, and he responded by trying to copy the lines of David's form in his journal. Though the lines in his stick drawing didn't resemble the proportions before him, to his father it was an enchanting moment. As the son studied the famous sculpture, the father studied the son. In that moment, both sets of eyes were opened to new possibilities.

. . .

"I'm not a girly girl," Annie confided, "but when I tried on that first dress, it fit so perfectly and I looked so beauti- ful . . ." Her words trailed off when her vocabulary failed her.

Earlier that day, Annie had gone shopping for her wed- ding dress in Cedar Rapids, Iowa. Her fiancé, stationed in Guantanamo Bay, Cuba, could only imagine what his bride- to-be would look like on that day, but Annie's mother and sisters didn't have to—they sat outside the dressing room, eagerly awaiting each new dress.

Hope's Bridal is located in a barn outside the city, and it is a must-stop for local brides. While there, Annie tried on a number of dresses until she found a strapless gown "that was so like me" that she felt sure it was the one.

Encouraging her to try it on and wear it around the showroom, the savvy salesperson placed a veil on Annie's head and turned the lights down so she could see the dress sparkle as it would during the evening glow of her wedding ceremony.

Annie turned and watched her mother inhale deeply, then audibly gasp. Her sister, Suzi, was speechless, but the tears pooling in Suzi's eyes confirmed Annie's thoughts.

This was the dress for her.

MOMENTS THAT SURPRISE US
Wonder.

Joy.

Beauty.

These feelings can ambush our senses at any time, any place. We're minding our own business, walking the dog, paying bills, or watching TV, and there is a moment of extraordinary clarity. It can happen while standing on the floor of Yosemite Valley or crossing an intersection in downtown Toledo.

It comes.

The moment is a sound—a symphony or a favorite rock band—transporting us from the concert hall to a place we've never been.

The moment is a feeling—so intensely arousing that the kiss, the touch, will be remembered long after the relationship is gone.

The moment is a taste—of a food or drink so splendidly flavored that we will forever seek another bite of chocolate or another sip of wine to re-create the experience.

The moment is creative—the geyser of ideas that bursts forth can't be stopped by man or environment.

The moment is spiritual—it's as if God has pulled back the curtain just for us, and revealed a glimpse of eternity and our purpose in it.

And then,

just like that,

the moment is gone.

Like seeing trees in a black night made violently visible by a flash of lightning, we're awed by these kinds of moments. We want more of them. There is something so powerful, so transcendent in these extreme moments that we're convinced that if we can latch onto them, we can harness their power to provide eternal happiness here and now.

"Beauty is only the promise of happiness," writes the nineteenth-century French author known as Stendhal.[1]

During and immediately after the breath-halting experience, we feel radiant. And we're thankful.

"Oh, God!" we gasp. But what we mean is, "Thank you beyond words for letting me have this moment." These moments are merely a taste. As long as the taste lingers, we are thankful for the experience.

But once we swallow, once the taste no longer lingers, our gratitude fades. We remember, but we no longer feel the experience, no longer smell the fragrance of the moment. Our prayers move from gratitude to entitlement. We deserve more.

Those rare moments leave us empty, with a hunger that we spend the rest of our lives trying to fill.

Prayers of Beauty and Wonder

If the first response to an intense experience that captivates mind, body, and soul is a prayer of thank-you, then undoubtedly the second and third responses will be "more" and "again."

Like the old Life Savers commercial where the boy watches the sun set and turns to his grandfather and says, "Do it again, Grandpa," we want to relive, repeat, and resume those incredible moments of beauty in our lives.

We salivate over thoughts of a past mouthwatering meal.

We lightly trace a finger across our lips as we remember that first kiss.

We inhale deeply, breathing in scents as if they had power to transport us to the original experience.

We desire these moments to go on forever. We want to command our senses to recall them on demand. But time and distance are the enemies of epiphanies.

In a tax-season stupor, David looked around his accounting office and took inventory. Standard office furniture, including a desk, a bookshelf, a couple of chairs, and a small sofa, were adorned with bobble-head dolls, miscellaneous company awards, and mugs with client logos. Dated pictures of his son in football gear, Halloween costumes, and Christmas card photos were displayed in disparate frames. And in the middle, a picture of the Italian countryside.

Tuscany.

It was a picture his wife had taken on their last trip. As he stared at the photo, he was disappointed, but not in the composition. The photo revealed a lush, bright green countryside speckled with dark green vineyards, framed by a brilliant blue sky and lit by a lemon yellow sun. The photo was fine, as far as photos go. David's disappointment came because, standing in his sixth-floor office in Atlanta, he couldn't smell the trees, feel the breeze, or hear the sounds of the elderly Italian men arguing in the village square. The things that tantalized his senses when the photo was originally made were no longer present. The photo was such a pale representation of actually being in the Tuscan countryside that even the most basic sensory details were lost. It was useless—David couldn't relive his vacation. The photo couldn't reclaim the moment.

Annie, like most brides, can tell you where she was, what she was wearing, and who she was with the moment she first fell in love—with her wedding dress. With an estimated 2.3 million weddings in the United States each year, and an average of $800 spent on each bride's dress, bridal gowns add a healthy $1.8 billion a year to the wedding industry. Whether she shops at Goodwill or Vera Wang, whether the dress has lace linings or layers of satin or is adorned with beads—a girl knows when she has found the perfect dress.

"Oh, it's so beautiful," she gushes.

Admiring friends and family members reinforce her choice, both at the store and later at the church: "You look so beautiful."

And she does.

Yet after the big day, most brides take this perfect garment—this once-in-a-lifetime dress she spent weeks shopping for, the very dress that enhanced her beauty on the most important day of her life—box it up, and store it in the attic.

Why?

If the dress is such a thing of wonder and so enhances the beauty of the young woman who wears it, why doesn't she wear it again?

Wearing it while buying a new car might help her negotiate a lower price with the dealer, and it's likely she'd move to the front of the line at the post office while dressed in white lace. If she's running late for work, the gown's plunging neckline could be helpful in talking her way out of a speeding ticket or getting her boss to overlook her tardiness.

Wearing the dress for other special occasions, such as a high school reunion or an important presentation at work, might help her feel as special, beautiful, and confident as she did on her wedding day. At the very least, pulling it out of the box on her anniversary and wearing it to dinner and a movie with her husband might help both of them recreate the joy of their wedding day.

But these suggestions are ridiculous. The feelings she had on her wedding day can't be re-created by wearing a dress. The moment has passed, and wearing the dress won't make it happen again. The experience lives in the moment, not in the dress.

Nate's world rocked under his feet as he watched his wife give birth to their first child. Just as Nora was about to be born, the midwife stepped aside and let Nate lift his daughter into the world. Nora took her first breath in Nate's arms.

He gazed down at her. Wet and wrinkled. Kicking at the air. The baby caught hold of his index finger, thick, creased, and stained with axle grease. But what caught his attention was *her* fingernails: tiny, perfect, and complete.

"You are so beautiful." He stared at her eyelashes. Her elegant lips. "Oh, God, you are so beautiful."

Nora cried, and then as suddenly as it happened, the moment passed. Nate handed his daughter to a hovering nurse. Once again an ordinary man, he felt awkward and out of place in the hospital delivery room—but forever changed by the beauty and awe of that moment. "Oh, God, thank you."

Experiencing a Broadway show can never be repeated in another theater. Though it's the same script, the same music, and in some cases, a more talented (though less star-studded) cast, it's not the same experience.

Moved by a film on the big screen, we rent the DVD to share the experience with friends and family—but the jokes aren't quite as funny, the vistas aren't as grand, and stunts aren't as daring. We can't relive them.

A birth.

A wedding.

A vacation in Italy.

A moment of discovery while watching a show.

"More!" we beg.

"Again!" we plead.

We use language to call forth more of the same, but we also use our actions. We return to the same beach at sunset, hoping for the same magical view; to the same relationship, hoping for the once-experienced intimacy; or to the same book for new insight into old problems. But these props do little to help us re-create the joy, wonder, and beauty found in the original supernatural event.

We're left only with our prayers for more.

"OH, GOD!"

In moments of extreme beauty, awe, wonder, or joy, we are overwhelmed by the sheer intensity of the experience. The burst of language during and immediately after such flashes is likely to be primal.

Why is it that our initial response is so often punctuated by the same two monosyllabic words?

"Oh, God."

Whether blurted out, whispered, or begged, calling out to God in sudden experiences of intense and surprising pleasure is as instinctive as crying out to God in moments of terror, confusion, or pain.

"Oh, my God!" we cry when we watch two great towers collapse into mountains of debris; but we also say it every Thanksgiving, crumbs spilling from our mouths as we savor Aunt Ruby's pumpkin pie.

The melody of a pennywhistle rising above the patriotic song of a marching band makes us weep for God and country.

Those words are a consistent response, but what do we mean when we invoke the name of God?

Is it just a cultural expression said without intention, without meaning?

Or is it a feeble attempt to make a connection with the Divine?

Why do we cry out to God?

Why not to Merlin, Buddha, or even Bob?

Perhaps because, whether intentional or not, conscious or not, our first instinct during intense moments is to cry out to God. Nate wasn't a believer, but when he saw his daughter, the words "Oh, God" slipped out without a second thought. There is something about the intensity of these moments that causes both believers and nonbelievers to acknowledge a higher power, if only for a moment.

When we can't control our experiences directly, we cry out to *God*, hoping he is the magic conduit through which we can re-create or relive those experiences. Whether deliberately or involuntarily, we cry out because we want control over the beauty and wonder we've experienced; and when we realize we don't have control, we turn to the only One who does.

"Oh, God!" isn't just a slip of the tongue. It's a cry for more from the only One who can give us more of these extraordinary moments.

WHERE IS GOD FOUND?
Is God only found in the extraordinary?

Or can he be found in the ordinary as well?

We don't notice every sunset with equal appreciation. We don't stop for every flower that opens its petals. And

204

we don't notice all the birds around us unless they have a distinctive song.

Why does a sunset at the beach or in the mountains seem sacred, yet every night we watch the same sun set from our bedroom window and we hardly notice?

Why do the flowers that bloom along our drive get less attention than the driver who cuts us off?

Why do we love the bird that sings outside our window but hate the one that nests in the dryer vent?

What if God resides equally in the ordinary as in the extraordinary? Why do we so frequently miss him in the ordinary and so often seek him in the extraordinary?

Maybe it has something to do with our expectations. We don't look for God in the ordinary because we don't expect to find him there. But the extraordinary? Ahh, that's where we expect to find God.

A wedding makes us search harder for the beauty in the moment as a way to redeem all of the preparation, time, and money that went into it. The view from the mountain is more intense because of the climb to get there. A baby is more beautiful because of the months of worry that preceded the birth.

Maybe intense moments are found in extraordinary circumstances because we're open to them.

What would happen if we were open to seeing God in the ordinary?

GOD IN THE ORDINARY

The idea of seeking God in the ordinary was first celebrated by the ancient Hebrews in the Old Testament. According to the Torah, God created the natural world and called it good;

then he delegated to humans the responsibility of caring for this jewel of his handiwork. The Jews built on this conviction, developing elaborate feasts at which they enjoyed food and drink in acts of worship.

Ordinary objects—meat, bread, and wine—became tangible reminders of the great things God had done. The spiritual and the physical joined in a sacred act. This tradition continues today during the celebration of Holy Communion, a ritualistic observance of one man giving his life (the physical) for another man's soul (the spiritual). Those who participate in this act recognize a value that goes beyond tasting, chewing, and swallowing; there is a divine connection found in the ordinary.

Maybe that is why God repeats himself in ordinary ways. He makes the sun rise, the roses bloom, and the birds sing—not once, but an infinite number of times. God is the master of "more" and "do it again."

G. K. Chesterton puts it this way in his classic book called *Orthodoxy*:

> The thing I mean can be seen . . . in children, when they find some game that they specifically enjoy. A child kicks his legs rhythmically through excess, not absence, of life. Because children have abounding vitality, because they are in spirit fierce and free, therefore they want things repeated and unchanged. They always say, "Do it again" and the grown-up person does it again until he is nearly dead. For grown-up people are not strong enough to exult in monotony.
>
> But perhaps God is strong enough to exult in

monotony. It is possible that God says every morning, "Do it again" to the sun; and every evening "Do it again" to the moon. It may not be automatic necessity that makes all daisies alike; it may be that God makes every daisy separately, but has never got tired of making them.[2]

Jesus took delight in the wonders of this world. He showed no hesitation in using physical props such as water, seeds of grain, wind, and soil to illustrate truths about God. Repeatedly, he associated sacred things with down-to-earth, common things.

Jesus relished his experiences of human pleasure and embraced them as intentionally as he chose the experience of human suffering. He developed a reputation for enjoying good food with friends. Several stories in the Gospels have as their backdrop a meal taken in the home of a friend, or even a foe.

Jesus' first miracle took place at a wedding banquet. When the wine ran out, Jesus created more, using the water in large washing pots as his raw material. And the result was not cheap wine, but vintage. The miracle was an act of generosity for the guests and a face-saving mercy for the host. Those who witnessed the miracle saw the extraordinary emerge from the ordinary.[3]

For Jesus and the early Christians, the mysteries of God were easily and naturally wrapped in the ordinary things of life. Jesus was resurrected not as a disembodied spirit but as a new man still capable of enjoying a meal of fried fish beside the lake with his friends. He was the ultimate combination of sacred and ordinary.

We see God in the extraordinary, but when we look for him in the ordinary, we find him there, too.

MOUNTAINTOP EXPERIENCES

The ancient Celts of Ireland and Scotland associated spiritual experiences with specific geographical locations: a deep, cold cave, a grove of ancient trees on a hilltop, an open meadow between thick forests, or a stubborn, jagged cliff enduring the rage of ocean waves. Through the sublime places of nature, the Celts believed we might glimpse the wonder of supernature. They believed these beautiful places had a kind of magical power to turn mundane life into mystical rapture.

The Gaelic word for these sacred spaces is *caol ait*. It means "thin places"—where the barrier between our world and the realm of the spirit is translucent. Thin places serve as holes in a fence where human beings can touch God and in return be touched by him. In thin places, anything can happen; these places are approached with a sense of anticipation.

Jesus climbed a mountain with three of his closest followers: Peter, James, and John. There, something extraordinary happened. Jesus suddenly appeared covered with radiant light, a light that seemed otherworldly, as if Jesus himself were a window through whom a brilliant light shone. As the trio watched, Jesus conversed with Moses and Elijah—great heroes of their faith. Then, as suddenly as it came, the glory passed, and Jesus was again alone with his three bewildered friends.

Once Peter collected himself, he suggested building a religious shrine on the spot to commemorate this moment of wonder. He believed it could become a famous place of pilgrimage, a place where people could further their faith and reflect on the wonder of heaven.

Jesus rejected the idea. Without further comment, he called the three disciples to follow him down the mountain, back to the tedious work of doing good in the world through provision, pardon, healing, deliverance, and hope.[4]

For a brief moment, heaven's wonder and power had come crashing through to this world, and the three observers had caught a glimpse of Jesus' true identity and his destiny. Jesus and his friends were offered only a glimpse of this intense pleasure in the most ordinary circumstances—standing in the middle of nowhere, hanging out in the ordinariness of life. And Jesus answered their prayers to acknowledge this dazzling moment of beauty by leading them back to the ordinary. He knew that the flash was of a world his friends couldn't live in, at least not yet.

Was this a *caol ait*—a thin place?

What if the freakish, wild, and uncontrolled moments of beauty, awe, and wonder we experience are *thin points* in time?

Rather than God responding to our cries for control, could it be that these responses—crying out to God and begging for more—are our responses to *his* call?

Could these prayers have been placed deep inside of us, triggering our brains to respond when called forth by a specific stimulus?

When teased with joy, are we hardwired to ask for more?

Are moments of wonder, joy, beauty, and insight God's little game of cat and mouse, teasing us with a taste of him, stoking an unquenchable hunger for more?

More of him?

THE RISK OF THE EXTRAORDINARY

In *Perelandra*, part of C. S. Lewis's space trilogy, the hero,
Ransom, is sent from earth to Venus, an Eden-like world
recently filled with life. Ransom's assignment is to resist
Weston, who has traveled to Venus to tempt the untainted
inhabitants to break the one prohibition set down by the
Creator. The world Ransom finds is lush, strange, and
unimaginably perfect, though utterly distinct from Earth.

Early after his arrival, Ransom happens upon a forest
filled with what he comes to call bubble trees. On the ends
of each branch, a small bubble begins to bud and grow
until its size and weight cause it to burst. As Ransom stands
beneath one of these trees, he is suddenly drenched from
the spray of a bursting bubble. The aroma is exquisite,
awakening his senses so that for a moment he seems aware
and able to absorb all the pleasure around him. Ecstasy. But
then the rapture passes.

Ransom is tempted to rush into the heart of the wood and
stand beneath a bubble tree and repeat the thrill again and
again. But something checks this temptation. In that perfect
world, intentionally repeating an accidental pleasure somehow cheapens the gift.

Our world suffers from the same fate. There is danger in
attempting to manufacture and repeat moments of ecstasy.
In our efforts to recreate the pleasure we've experienced at
God's hand, we pervert it with our own touch.

- We want to remember the experience of our first kiss,
  but in our efforts to hunt down and capture the feeling,
  we become addicted to pornography.
- A moment of insight and understanding makes us

forget our limitations. We try to manufacture feelings of confidence, strength, and energy through artificial means, and we end up as drug addicts or alcoholics.

- An effort to find comfort in food leads to eating addictions.
- A desire to be important leads to codependent behavior.
- The lust for external beauty results in a scalpel to our skin.

Whenever we try to control and manipulate the pleasure God gives us, we pervert it. That's why he rarely allows us to repeat those moments. Instead, he chooses to answer our prayers for "more" and "again" with new surprises.

Even if our attempts to re-create or relive peak experiences don't result in perversion, we still can't manufacture those moments ourselves, just like we can't tickle ourselves. We giggle, laugh, or scream with joy when someone else tickles us, but when we try to tickle ourselves, we get little sensory response. Scientists say this happens because the brain anticipates self-touches; it is only when someone else touches us that our brain is surprised. When we try to tickle ourselves, our bodies adjust and respond accordingly; as a result, we can't be surprised at our own tickle.

In intense moments, the joy, like an unexpected touch, is found in the fact that it comes when we weren't anticipating it.

That's also why we can never capture, imprison, and own the intensity of such experiences. We can't bottle them, put them on the shelves as trophies, or pull them out as treasures we've stashed away. Try as we might, it appears that God's gifts of joy will not be *possessed* in this world.

We can't control the moment.

But perhaps *control* isn't the idea.

THE BIG TEASE

Maybe there is another purpose behind these experiences.

Perhaps these moments of beauty and joy are intended for God's purposes rather than our own.

Maybe he is deliberately providing us with overwhelming experiences we can't provide for ourselves in an effort to ruin us from ever being content with life here on earth. Maybe he wants us to have an eternal desire for more.

Maybe he buried the primal prayer of "Thanks, but I want more" deep inside of us to burst forth in response to such transcendent occasions so that our desire for more will cause us to seek him more.

We intuitively recognize that the Creator of those moments is the only one who can deliver them, so naturally we look to him for more. Could it be that he intended it that way?

Like one more turn at the game, or one more listen to a favorite book, it's not the object that brings the pleasure; it's the interaction. We all want confirmation that we're special, that we're loved, and that we're worthy of being heard.

These periodic intrusions of delight, these flashes of joy that, without warning, shatter the tedium of our lives and then run for cover, are used by God. An instant of beautiful, expanding, indescribable sensation could be more than purely a sensory pleasure. Maybe it is an acknowledgment that we're special, that we're part of something bigger than ourselves, and that we've experienced something to which we can lay claim but not capture.

In trying to reclaim these moments, we are seeking to meet God.

When we ask for more, we ask for more of him.

Our prayer for him to "do it again, Daddy" is a request to repeat our experience with him. When we casually say, "Oh, God," we're acknowledging instinctively something we may not be ready to acknowledge intellectually.

Knowing how dangerous and addictive wonder can be, how does God answer a prayer so obviously prompted by his own inducements? If these extraordinary moments truly represent divine connections, why are they not repeatable on demand?

Are we in danger of making the extraordinary simply ordinary?

Perhaps God prefers that we swim in the ordinary and only occasionally dip into the extraordinary, because there are huge risks for him in the extraordinary. God's risk in creating a world through which he can pass wonder, beauty, and joy is that we may fall in love with the creation rather than the Creator.

And we've certainly done that, even in our present, fallen world. The apostle Paul says it is sinful to honor the gift over the giver.[b] God could have planted us on a desolate rock—there are billions of them floating around the universe. Instead, he put us in the lap of green pastures and majestic mountains, a realm that should yield to us, but to which we so easily yield—most often by simply wanting more and more of one small piece of a vast treasure.

God answers our prayers of "more," "again," and "oh,

God," not with more of the same, but with reminders that "the same" is but a pale imitation of the real thing. Just as a bridal gown can't bring back the magic of the wedding day, and a photograph can't convey the smell of ripening grapes in the Italian countryside, the most wondrous moments of extraordinary beauty, joy, and insight—the thin points—are still only pale tactile reminders of the real mind-blowing experiences that only God can offer.

We don't experience every sunset the same, not because God doesn't want us to experience the joy and beauty of a particular one, but because the joy and the beauty weren't in the sunset any more than they were in the bridal gown.

When we try on the dress, look at the photo, or remember the birth, we're reminded that these are just symbols of the real thing. God doesn't repeat the same fingerprint, snowflake, or sunset, but he repeats the act of creation in an attempt to get us to see him, the Creator.

Our prayers for more are answered with hit-and-run experiences that stir our hunger, provoke us to prayer, and cause us to seek the source of the tantalizing goodness we have smelled cooking but have not yet tasted. When we experience beauty, joy, or wonder, when we're dazzled or awestruck, or when we experience new understanding, these are mere suggestions of what is yet to come.

Perhaps God resides in the ordinary while he sends us brief glimpses of an extraordinary life we're not yet prepared for. When we cry out for more, he answers our prayers, not by repeating the same painting, but by showing us glimpses of the palette from which all color comes.

God is in the ordinary and the extraordinary. The ordinary can even be extraordinarily beautiful—like a Thanksgiving dinner with all those crazy relatives, when for one moment, they all join hands, set aside their differences, and pray to someone bigger than themselves.

"Beauty is an ecstasy; it is as simple as hunger," writes Somerset Maugham in *Cakes and Ale*.[6] But unlike Charles Dickens's hungry orphan, Oliver Twist, who was fixated on getting a little more gruel from the master, God's answer to our prayer isn't more slop on our plate. God's answer is to increase our hunger—for him. His moments of beauty, insight, and wonder are just tastes of the banquet to come in eternity.

These are the six prayers God always answers: bargaining prayers, questioning prayers, prayers for justice, desperate prayers, audacious prayers, and prayers for beauty and happiness. God delights in answering these six prayers. But there is one more prayer God must answer. And even though he hates to answer it, he will.

10
THE PRAYER GOD HATES
TO ANSWER—BUT WILL

POSTERS DEFINED THE 1970S: the long, golden mane of Farrah Fawcett, the bare chest of Andy Gibb, and the kitten suspended by its paws from a tree limb, with the caption "Hang in there."

Though the images on the posters may have faded like the paper on which they were printed, there is a slogan from a poster that seems to have made permanent entrée into the cultural vernacular. Maybe you remember it.

Most versions of the poster have a picture of a bird flying through a blue sky, with words alongside in a scrolling font. But even if you haven't seen the poster, you've probably heard its message: "If you love something, set it free. If it comes back, it's yours. If it doesn't, it never was. . . ."

Thirty years later, humor Web sites are rife with new variations:

Pessimistic: If you love somebody, set her free. If she ever comes back, she's yours. If she doesn't, well, as expected, she never was.

Optimistic: If you love somebody, set her free. Don't worry, she'll come back.

Suspicious: If you love somebody, set her free. If she ever comes back, ask her why.

Playful: If you love somebody, set her free. If she comes back and if you love her still, set her free again, repeat.

Lawyer: If you love somebody, set her free. Clause 1a of paragraph 13a-1 in the second amendment of the Matrimonial Freedom Act clearly states that . . .

Bill Gates: If you love somebody, set her free. . . . If she comes back, I think we can charge her for reinstallation fees and tell her that she's also going to get an upgrade.

Psychologist: If you love somebody, set her free. If she comes back, her superego is dominant. If she doesn't come back, her id is supreme. If she doesn't go, she must be crazy.

Marketing: If you love somebody, set her free. If she comes back, she has brand loyalty. If she doesn't, reposition the brand in new markets. [1]

Some have taken these words and applied them to new contexts:

If you love something, set it free.
If it comes back, it will always be yours.

If it doesn't come back, it was never yours to begin with.
But, if it just sits in your living room,
messes up your stuff, eats your food,
uses your telephone, takes your money
and doesn't appear to realize that you had set it free . . .
You either married it or gave birth to it.[2]

No one really turns to these cheesy principles for real relationship advice, right?

In the twenty-first century, a poster isn't limited to describing something you hang on the wall. A poster can also describe those who post messages online. And it seems the "Dear Abby" poster of the seventies has now attracted online posters.

Looking for answers, Darkest_angel0o posted this appeal on a Yahoo message board:

> You know how they say, if you love something let it go, if it comes back it was always yours, and if it doesn't it was never yours? What if you let it go, and it comes back, and you have to let it go again?
>
> Seriously . . . you can only let something go so many times.

Taking her question seriously, a number of people posted responses.

> **CNT:** Once you let it go, leave it alone. If it comes back then they will just do it to you all over again because they think they can.

Morriskat1 40: Move on, you are wasting precious time you could be making good memories with someone else.

Mike: Can I answer your question with a question of my own, please? What if someone let you go AFTER you begged, cried, and pleaded with them to not let you go. What then? I mean, if someone whom your heart belongs to decided to let you free, even though you said you DID NOT want to be set free? What then?

Sakura: Tough call, but if it goes and it came back, that should be it. If it goes again . . . as you said, you can only let it go so many times. My boyfriend has just dumped me after cheating on me, but I still love him, and there is still a chance of him coming back.

The Web site allows readers to vote for the best answer, and they did. The winning response was from Soccerlvr4life: "If u cant stand letting it go again then dont let it come back." Though no official prize was given for gut-wrenching honesty, we'd award the title to Meghan, who simply responded, "Uhhhhh . . . I don't know."[3]

Setting aside the obvious—that Darkest_angel0o is seeking relationship advice from people who can't spell, based on a dubious principle found on a decades-old poster—the responses seem to suggest that as a people we have trouble with loving.

And letting go.

TO KNOW YOU

There are an infinite number of things we want to know:

> I want to know where my car keys are.
> I want to know who is in charge!
> I want to know how much it costs.
> I want to know what's on the test.
> I want to know what you want.

But perhaps more than we want to know, we want to be known.

Cheers was a popular sitcom in the 1980s. It took place in a bar, and the appeal was found in a set of characters who either worked at, or regularly frequented, the watering hole. Together, they formed their own community, a sort of dysfunctional family.

For each character, the bar represented something more than a place to get a drink. The opening song said it best: "Where everybody knows your name." But more than your name, *Cheers* was a place where everybody knew *you*.

This feeling is re-created in local coffee shops today. Whether in a national chain or in an independent, both of us—Mark in Minneapolis and Jennifer in Atlanta—have spent hours in coffee shops writing, and day after day, we've observed the same people coming in.

It could be the coffee, but perhaps it's something else.

A familiar customer walks in, and the barista begins to prepare the customer's favorite mocha latte even before she orders. After a few minutes of chitchat with the staff and the other regulars, she leaves sipping hot coffee, warmed by the community she's found. People return to their favorite spots, not only because they like the coffee, but because they like being known.

When we talk about knowing "in the biblical sense," we often use the phrase as a euphemism for sex, as in "Adam knew Eve." But like most biblical words, the phrase "to know" has greater depth and meaning than the surface reveals. When the Bible talks about Adam "knowing" Eve, it uses the Hebrew word *yada*. The writer could have chosen other words, such as *yashav* ("*to lie with*"), or even the verb *bo*, which means "*to enter*." But the writer specifically chose the verb *to know*.

In the days of the ancient Hebrews, *knowledge* wasn't considered just a list of data or facts. Knowledge was experiential. So when the writer uses the word *yada*, he is talking about something more than "lying with" Eve or "entering" Eve; he is talking about an intimate knowledge—an *experience* of Eve.

When Adam knew Eve, he did more than have sex with her; he experienced every part of her. He understood her. He felt her physically and emotionally. Sex is a physical intimacy, but Adam was also intimate with Eve in ways that transcended sexuality.

He knew her.

There is perhaps only one other relationship more intimate than a husband and wife, and that is the relationship between a pregnant woman and the child she carries. Her breath is her baby's breath. Her heartbeat ensures his heartbeat. From the first flutter in her belly, to the moment he leaves the birth canal, she intimately experiences her child. His very survival depends on her.

She knows her child.

SIX PRAYERS GOD ALWAYS ANSWERS

In the ancient book of Jeremiah, there is an interesting note from God. In the first chapter, God says, "Before I formed you in the womb I knew you . . ."[4] The word choice here is important.

God says, "I *yada*'d you."

I experienced you fully.

I knew you.

God is more intimate with us than the mother whose breath and heartbeat were inextricably tied to her own baby. God knew us.

And we knew him.

But . . .

And this is a big "but."

But, once we entered the world, the choice to know him—as intimately as he knew us—became ours.

Free WILL

Christians might argue that the greatest gift we received from God was the gift of his Son, who died on a cross to save us from our sins. But perhaps that wasn't the greatest gift.

To accept the Cross as the greatest gift, to be the recipient of salvation, one has to choose to believe in the saving power of Jesus at the Cross. Without making the choice, it is an unopened gift.

Perhaps the greatest gift God has given us isn't the Cross. It could be that the greatest gift from God is free will—the ability to choose. He had the option to create us as automatons doing and saying whatever it is that he preprogrammed us to do and say. But he didn't. He made us in his image, with the ability to choose what *we will* at every step.

God is so intent on securing our freedom that he doesn't even hardwire us to believe in his existence. Nature hints at Divine design. For those who wish to see it that way, the odds are incalculable that all earth's contingencies should stack up as they do, to provide just the right environment for life.

But agnosticism can seem reasonable, too, when presented by a competent skeptic. For those who choose not to believe in God, there is no obvious and literal presence of him in the measurable world. We don't know God exists the way we know that maple trees in Vermont exist.

Hard scientific evidence that God exists is at best a 50/50 prospect.

Either view of life requires faith. Choose to believe certain evidence and ignore other evidence. God, it seems, has made it equally easy to believe and doubt.

Simple to trust.

Simple to walk away.

Jesus continued this tradition during his time on earth. Yes, there were blaring, mind-numbing miracles, but the miracles never ensured belief from those who witnessed them.

can I Have a wItness?

There once was a crazy man. This man was beyond the talking-to-yourself-not-showering-for-weeks kind of crazy. This man was so crazy he couldn't be restrained. The village had tried. He had even been chained hand and foot, but he tore the chains apart and broke the irons on his feet.[5] Night and day this man terrified people as he wandered the tombs and homes around the village, crying out and cutting himself with stones.

When he showed up, women grabbed their children, ran

inside, and locked the door. Men did too. No one was strong enough to subdue him. They believed he was possessed by evil spirits.

Jesus entered the village. The man sprinted directly toward him. Now, this would be enough to make a lesser man run. But Jesus saw him coming from a distance and waited until he came closer. He determined that the man was possessed. A quick conversation confirmed it.

Jesus commanded the evil spirits out of the man and sent them into a herd of pigs feeding on the hillside. The spirits left the man and entered the pigs. Before mad cow disease, there was mad pig disease. Two thousand pigs suddenly rushed down the steep bank to the lake and drowned. Those on the hillside could hardly believe what they saw, but if they needed confirmation that a miracle had taken place, the uncontrollable crazy man "was sitting there fully clothed and perfectly sane."[6]

Imagine seeing such a transformation on film. The visuals would be spectacular. One minute, two thousand pigs are grazing on the hillside; the next minute, pig carcasses cover the lake. First, the scary crazy man can't be restrained, and suddenly he's sitting, in pressed khakis and a navy blazer, drinking a latte.

It would have been a terrifying experience, something to tell the grandchildren. Surely everyone who saw it fell at the feet of Jesus and worshiped him, right?

Not exactly.

The next scene shows those who witnessed the miracle pleading with Jesus to leave. As Jesus climbs in the boat, the only one who wants him to stay is the once-crazy man, who is convinced Jesus transformed his life.

What about the others? Wasn't this proof enough for them?

We look at this miracle and the lack of village faith, and we ask ourselves, couldn't Jesus have said or done something differently to convince them?

In a separate story, a young man comes to Jesus with a question. "Good teacher," he asked, "what must I do to inherit eternal life?"[7]

Jesus responds with a question of his own. "Why do you call me good? Only God is truly good." He seems to be asking the man, "Do you know who you are addressing?" Then, without waiting for a reply, Jesus responds to the man's question. "Keep the commandments."

"Which ones?" the man asks.

It was a serious question. The Jews prescribed hundreds of laws covering every minute detail of life. Jesus steers clear of these traditions and focuses on six simple statements familiar to anyone who has read the Old Testament: "You shall not murder, you shall not commit adultery, you shall not steal, you shall not give false testimony, honor your father and mother, and love your neighbor as yourself." Jesus quotes five of the ten commands, plus one—a command to love.

The man answers, "All these I have kept."

"One thing you lack," Jesus adds. "Go sell your possessions and give to the poor. . . . Then follow me."

When the man hears Jesus' words, his face falls. He turns and fades away into the shadows of history.

And Jesus lets him go. He *lets* him go.

Couldn't Jesus have mustered an argument?

Couldn't he have performed a miracle to convince the man it would be worth it?

226

Certainly Jesus has the power to bend the man's will like a dieter to a chocolate donut! But the questions are academic. In dealing with this man, and with all humans, Jesus *invites*. He does not conscript. He offers this man a relationship. He asks for permission to know and be known. But he leaves the option open for the man to push aside the offer.

These are tragic scenes—a man walking away from intimacy with God, a crowd pleading with Jesus to leave. But it happens again and again, and God does nothing to stop it.

"There are two kinds of people in the end," wrote C. S. Lewis in his fantasy *The Great Divorce*. "Those who say, 'Thy will be done,' and those to whom God says, 'Thy will be done.'"[8] God cannot know those who choose not to be known. This seems to be a law he has woven so deeply into the order of the universe that even the love or sorrow he feels will not allow him to bend it.

In the 2003 movie *Bruce Almighty*, television reporter Bruce Nolan is given God's job complete with all of God's powers. But Bruce fails as miserably at being God as he does at being a boyfriend to the woman he loves. In a private moment with God, Bruce asks, "How do you make so many people love you without affecting free will?"

God, played by Morgan Freeman, snorts, "Heh, welcome to my world, son. If you come up with an answer to that one, let me know."

THESE BOOTS ARE MADE FOR WALKING
Talking to God can be foolish.

Talking to God can even be dangerous.

He says, "Ask and you will receive." It's a disclaimer and a warning, as well as a promise. We will get—in the extreme—exactly what we ask for. And there is the rub: Sometimes we'd be better off keeping our mouths shut.

Herman Melville's epic, *Moby Dick*, tells the tragic tale of the fated Nantucket whaling ship, the *Pequod*, skippered by the monomaniacal Captain Ahab. The novel weaves together many themes. But the anchor that holds it is the indomitable force of will and the doom that befalls those who refuse to be governed by anything but their own volition.

In the book, the grizzled Ahab convinces his crew to swear allegiance to his own private obsession—Ahab has vowed to hunt and kill the infamous white sperm whale, Moby Dick. On a previous voyage, the monster devoured his leg and left him physically and emotionally maimed. Ahab intends revenge.

But Ahab is so contorted with hatred that he believes Moby Dick to be the embodiment of Evil itself. In the dark crevices of madness, Ahab barters away his soul simply for the right to plunge a harpoon into the heart of this invincible behemoth. In a blasphemous prayer, Ahab denies and defies God, his own reason, and the lives of all his men. He demands that his Creator leave him alone to battle the monster his way, in his own strength. His prayer is granted.

The end is not what Ahab imagines. In the tragic climax, Ahab does battle Moby Dick without any aid of benevolent Providence. Yet instead of vanquishing the whale, Ahab is himself plunged into the depths of the sea.

Standing alone was the fate he desired.

He gets that, and horribly more.

America celebrates independent heroes. From John Wayne to Thoreau to Donald Trump to popular rap singers, we celebrate the defiant voice. We are a cowboy people, idolizing those who take to the range in need of nothing and no one. We reward self-determination at all costs. We make them obscenely wealthy. We defend self-expression in any form. If there is an individual will, there is an individual way. And oh, is there ever a will . . . 300 million of them!

Violet Beauregarde got exactly what she wanted. In Roald Dahl's novel *Charlie and the Chocolate Factory* (and its subsequent film adaptations), Violet is the world-record gum-chewing champion for chomping the same piece of gum three months straight. On a tour through Willy Wonka's candy factory, Wonka warns Violet not to touch the "Three Meal Gum" because it hasn't been perfected and might cause unanticipated side effects. Violet, however, can't resist.

When she sees the colorful gum ball, she grabs it and stuffs it into her mouth. As she chews, she experiences the sensations of three full meals: breakfast, lunch, dinner. But when she gets dessert—it's blueberry pie—something horrid happens. Violet Beauregarde turns into a colossal blueberry. Willy Wonka sighs, then gives the order that she should be rolled off to the juicing room and pressed before she explodes.

The moral in Dahl's delightful and penetrating story is poignant: We had better watch our wishes, for they can come true in the most literal ways. But perhaps there is another moral here: Sometimes the thing we want most can take us away from the one who created it.

In choosing the gum over Wonka's warning, Violet has essentially separated herself from the candy maker forever.

Street-level theology is that pure and that simple.

Ask.

Receive.

No matter what you ask.

We can actually pray prayers that drive us away from God.

And he answers those prayers.

Prayers questioning God's existence, prayers calling for justice, and prayers of desperation sometimes elicit answers so surprisingly subtle we may pass them by or label them chance.

Yet they are answered.

Always.

Completely.

But the principle is dangerously consistent, even when we demand to be left alone. Here, too, we are given what we ask for.

Strange, isn't it?

The sword cuts both ways. We're quite free to say anything to him we wish. And whatever we say, the promise holds: "Ask and you will receive."

Jerry Cruncher, the rascally grave robber in Charles Dickens's *Tale of Two Cities*, understood this principle. In the book, he beats his saintly wife for praying. He believes her prayers impede his prosperity. Cruncher knows the power of prayer—though he certainly doesn't like it.

"Leave me alone" is a dangerous prayer. For some classical Calvinists, Muslims, Buddhists, and those who believe in scientific determination, this prayer isn't threatening—it's meaningless. In those philosophies, the world runs either in an unbroken chain of causes and effects or as an ordained order governed by some unmovable Mover. Nothing changes anything anyway, they believe, so whatever will be, will be.

But if God gives us free will, asking to be left alone has deadly consequences. Free will says we can pray for whatever we wish, even for God to leave us alone. Free will says God must answer this prayer too.

What kind of God would permit such defiance?

Any parent of a two-year-old knows if you don't win the battle of wills, you're only asking for long-term trouble. Surely, as the unnamed writer of the book of Hebrews claims, God is a parent who disciplines the children he loves.[9]

But God seems to run a pretty footloose household. His children run about demanding and getting their way, at least for a season. Why would God take such a laissez-faire approach to parenting? Is he a lazy parent who stands by while right under his nose his kids smoke crack, steal retirement funds, abuse his other children, and doom themselves to an eternal existence of unspeakable misery?

It is a serious question: Why doesn't God put his house in better order?

Why does he let us crawl under the sink and swallow poison?

Wouldn't any father worth his salt step in and put a halt to our self-destruction, especially given the extremely long-term ramifications of our choices?

Surely he must be as frustrated by the question as we are. God grants us the dignity of bending his ear with the intent of turning his hand one direction and not another. But our free will means that God must make room for wills beyond his own. Through prayer, we exercise our will, seeking to have God change his. It's a free-for-all universe where anything might happen.

Nearly everything does.

But once we embrace the notion that God actually and genuinely communicates, and that he might even adjust his course of action based on our request, prayer becomes an exciting adventure. An adventure with choices.

If God gives humans the right to embrace a relationship with him, then he must give us the right to unlock the gate and walk away from that same relationship. If we do, God must let us go. If he didn't, then a supposed relationship with him would turn out to be meaningless.

To *know* means giving us the option to *go*.

Gone Forever?

By offering us an authentic option to stay or stray, God gambles on us. Given the human hankering (that he gave us, no less) to "go it alone," God must put his own heart on the auction block. He chooses the possibility of disappointment—even his own loneliness—as the price for the potential of love.

He's God, so not only does he know everything that is, but he must also grieve everything that might have been. There must be infinite joy, just as there must be infinite sadness, in being God.

Mark was twelve and visiting his uncle's home in Ohio when he was awakened by a presence in the room. There, in what felt like an audible voice, God asked him if he would spend his life communicating the Gospel. It came as a question, not a command. Mark understood immediately what it meant. He was to be a preacher.

But Mark's teen years brought confusion and resistance to what he knew was his destiny. He had witnessed firsthand the tedium and conflict involved in parish ministry. His father led a small church in Northern California, and during one church business meeting, Mark listened while an elder publicly took his father to task for hiring a youth pastor instead of relying on volunteers. It was an ugly scene. After the meeting, Mark looked at his dad and vowed, "I'll never do what you're doing."

For ten years, Mark walked away from God's call. He told himself he would do anything for God—anything except be a pastor. This caveat set him adrift. He moved from job to job, without direction. Then one night, he felt the heavy weight of confusion, and he prayed, "God, what's wrong with me? Why can't I find my place? What do you want me to do?"

A small Bible sat on a table near him. Mark felt an urge to open it. As he did, his eyes fell on these words in Paul's letter to the Colossians: "Be sure to carry out the ministry the Lord gave you."[10]

"What ministry?"

His imagination reignited with the memory of his encounter in Ohio. He remembered God's directive. He remembered his response. "You have rejected your call," said an inner voice. Mark conceded. Two months later, he accepted a position to pastor a small church in central California.

According to the biblical book that bears his name, God commissioned Jonah to carry a message to a wicked and about-to-be doomed city—Nineveh. Jonah heard the call. Then he calculated the sorry life expectancy of those who embrace the prophetic mantle. Weighing the balance, Jonah ran in the opposite direction.

God let him run.

He let him run far.

Jonah got his wish. He was given the freedom to disobey God.

But God did not make Jonah's running an easy journey. He put pressure on him every step of the way. When Jonah hopped a ship to sail across the Mediterranean, God sent a storm. When the sailors onboard understood the storm was a curse from God, they threw Jonah overboard at his request. God then sent a giant Leviathan to swallow Jonah and take him as deep as the ocean itself.

Jonah was given the freedom to run, but it was no picnic at the beach.

For three days, Jonah sat in the acid bath of a whale's stomach, digesting his fate and weighing his options. Maybe it was time to change his choice? Maybe it was time to repent, submit, and obey God? Maybe he should let God *know* him?

Nothing mandated this change—except perhaps, the inconvenience of living out the bitter ramifications of his defiance. Jonah weighed the implications and decided God's commission might not be so bad after all. He prayed and recanted his rebellion. The monster spewed him onto the beach and back on the road to Nineveh. God heard and answered Jonah's second prayer just as he had heard his first prayer to run.

If God gives us the ultimate freedom to walk our own way, it doesn't mean that God has to make that choice easy. After all, we are created in God's image. If we have a will to be stubborn, God has a will to be stubborn as well. If we seem determined, God is more so. And while he honors our option to defy him and walk away from relationship, he tenaciously works within his laws of freedom to counter our self-destructive autonomy.

Moses was flat-out defiant when God first commissioned him to go to Egypt and liberate the Hebrews from slavery.

"Why me?" Moses objected. "I stutter and can't speak."

"Not a problem," answered God. "I can fix that."

"No, you don't want me. Send my brother Aaron instead. He's a smooth talker, and Pharaoh is bound to listen to him. Not me . . ."

Moses exercises his right to say no, but God doesn't take "no" easily. He performs a couple of miracles for Moses just to prove his power. Moses is impressed, but retorts, "Ah, just send Aaron instead."

This time God gets angry. "I was going to heal your speech impediment, but since you clearly don't want that, I will send Aaron—as your spokesman. You go, and Aaron will be your voice."[11]

God is persistent, and finally, Moses concedes.

Gideon, in the book of Judges, was equally reluctant to take up an assignment from God. Israel was suffering under the oppression of Midianite raiders. God needed a champion who could lead the resistance. So he went to the smallest tribe, the weakest clan, and found the youngest boy in the family—Gideon—and revealed his plan. This is God's favorite strategy—take the wrong man and a dumb plan and see what happens.

Gideon hesitates, to say the least. He stalls for time and scrambles for a way to deny God his agenda. He finally responds to God's initiative with a series of tests through which God can prove that he is really God and his plans are legitimate. Gideon is groping for an excuse to disregard God.

But God doesn't take no easily. God accommodates Gideon's persistent skepticism and testing, making it difficult for Gideon to disobey. In the end, Gideon sees that life will be easier risking danger with God than hiding from him.[12]

This isn't some sort of arm-twisting, but like Mark and Jonah, Moses and Gideon found their discomfort gave them a chance to reflect, change their mind, and reconsider their first impulse. God grants not only the seventh chance to change our mind and return, but the seventy-times-seven chance. His gift, once rejected, can be reclaimed as long as we walk this earth.

THE PRICE OF LOVE

We can run from God.

We can continue to run. But it's not easy.

It's not easy to follow God either.

Those who seek the path of least pain may find both choices painful. However, God's persistence gives us time to tease out competing motivations and fears. Do we desire to follow God but we're afraid of his path, or are we saying no, no matter what? God recognizes the difference and responds appropriately.

Jesus told a story about a shepherd with one hundred sheep. Overnight, one of the lambs wanders off. "What does the shepherd do?" Jesus asks.

He leaves the ninety-nine and goes in search of the lost lamb.[13] God's heart is to rescue us from our wayward choices. He will search for us, he will find us, but like the prodigal son, it's up to us to make the decision to come home. When we do, restoration is waiting.

Free will is the price of real love. It can also be the dangerous downside of a universe where prayers can be answered.

God allows separation.

And he will allow it forever.

"How can a good God send people to hell?" we ask.

It's a hard question. But it is less confusing if we think not of God sending people away, but of people choosing to walk away.

God wants companionship. He seeks conversation and partnership in the universe. God made us for this purpose and knows we cannot live well without relationship with him. He has even made his friendship possible and easily accessible if we request it.

He asks for our allegiance.

He desires our hearts.

Not that he might own us, but that he might love and be loved.

You fascinate God.

If in our desperation we call to him, he will come. But if in our resolution we demand independence, he will release us. The last thing he wants is to lock his children in the basement of heaven when what they want is to escape.

God waits, but he does not wait forever.

Graham Greene wrote his novel, *The End of the Affair*, just months before he renounced atheism to embrace Christianity. The novel is roughly autobiographical. Set in Britain in the 1940s, the story contrasts the love one man has for a woman and the bitter loneliness that follows him when she finally turns her love to God. In the end the battered protagonist, a stubborn atheist, is forced to admit God's existence. His confession comes, however, not from love, but from exhaustion and hatred. After the death of the woman he so passionately loved, he cries out, "O God, You've done enough. You've robbed me of enough, I'm too tired and old to learn to love, leave me alone for ever."[14]

It is a prayer God must answer.

God wants to know us intimately, and he did before we were born, but once we hit the birth canal, the choices became all ours.

We can walk away.

And some do.

Forever.

A few verses after Matthew records Jesus saying, "Keep on asking, and you will receive what you ask for,"[15] Matthew also records Jesus saying, "Not everyone who calls out to me, 'Lord! Lord!' will enter the Kingdom of Heaven. Only those who actually do the will of my Father in heaven will enter. On judgment day many will say to me, 'Lord! Lord! . . . But I will reply, 'I never knew you. Get away from me, you who break God's laws.'"[16]

If he knew us, if he *yada*'d us in our mother's womb, is it possible that he could one day say he never knew us?

Though Matthew wrote in Greek, the word *knew (ginosko)* in "I never *knew* you" is clearly related to the Hebrew word *yada*. Jesus tells us there are some who will come to him and call him Lord, yet he won't have been intimate with them, he won't have experienced them. He will say to them, "I never knew you."

Jesus longs for us to be intimate with him.

To know us.

He wants that more than anything else.

But Jesus never forces himself on us.

In the book of Revelation, Jesus actually says, "Look! I stand at the door and knock. If you hear my voice and open the door, I will come in, and we will share a meal together as friends."[17] Even with believers, those who say, "Lord, Lord," Jesus won't crash down the door. He only comes in by invitation.

When he says, "Away from me," Jesus isn't being ugly; he's stating fact. "You didn't let me know you. I wasn't intimate with you."

God woos us.

He doesn't force himself on us.

So great is his respect for our will that he will let *us* decide.

Intimate Persuasion

God gives us freedom to walk with him or walk away from him.

He also gives us a chance to change our minds, but he doesn't wait forever.

Jane Austen's last completed novel, *Persuasion*, is a romance about second chances after regrettable choices. Anne Elliot is the middle daughter of Sir Walter Elliot, a baronet far too conscious of his comely pedigree and handsome face.

Eight years earlier, Anne fell deeply in love with the young Captain Frederick Wentworth. But Wentworth had no family connections and little prospect for provision.

Anne was persuaded by a neighbor to break the engagement.

Now, with Anne still a spinster and Wentworth having made his fortune as a merchant sailor, the captain returns to court another young girl in the district. But the story has a happy ending, and Anne and Captain Wentworth finally reunite.

Anne chose independence. But having lived without love, she tasted the price of solitude. When given the opportunity to recant, she humbles herself and embraces love. Presumably, the two second-chance lovers live happily ever after.

God hates our prayers for independence, but he loves us enough to answer them. But it is his desperate prayer that like the seventies poster, if he sets us free, we will come back to him.

11
"some were praying to a god they didn't even know"

STUDENTS, FACULTY, AND ALUMNI ALL AGREE that
Virginia Tech is a special place:

> The lush green grass of the drill field
> Stately old buildings formed from a medley of colored
> limestone
> The Blue Ridge Mountains rising in the background

These are the images that earned Virginia Tech the nick-
name "God's country." But on April 16, 2007, these images
were replaced by more gruesome pictures:

> Terrified students locked in classrooms or jumping out
> of windows
> Two young men holding a table against a door to keep
> a killer out

> Coeds sobbing as their silent cell phones awaited calls
> and text messages that never came

For thirty-two victims, their last image of the campus wasn't one of tranquility; it was of murder—by a fellow student with a gun.

Beginning in the initial hours of this tragedy, and continuing for the next few weeks, prayers were hurled, quietly whispered, begged in desperation, sung in groups, and simply exhaled when words failed.

A campus prayed.

So did a nation.

Bargains were exchanged: "God, if you let her live, I promise I will go to church."

Questions like, "God, why is this happening?" were quickly followed by selfish prayers: "Please keep *me* safe."

The grieving cried out to God for justice.

Desperate prayers were the norm: "God, help us!"

And when parents heard from their children, there were prayers of joy: "Thank God you're alive!"

Regardless of the shape and form, prayer was the conduit for reaching the One who could fix things. If you had been God on that day, you would have heard it all.

Heidi Weiss is a student in Georgia, but she was visiting her fiancé, Daniel Hager, on the Virginia Tech campus that April morning. She told *The Christian Index* that "at first everybody thought it was like what happened early in the fall semester when an escaped convict came on campus and shot and killed a sheriff's deputy and a security guard. The campus was shut down then and students were sent into locked-down dorms."[1]

But the students in the dorm soon learned that this situation was tragically worse. When they flipped on the TV, international news stations showed them what they couldn't see from their dorm windows.

If ever there was a need for prayer, this was it.

"We got the people in the dormitory together and prayed," said Heidi. Her fiancé, Daniel, regularly held Bible studies in the dorm. Though all were invited, the studies were usually attended by only ten or fifteen regulars. But that morning, everyone wanted to pray. "Some of the students consistently refused his invitations to attend, but everyone participated in this prayer meeting," said Heidi. "Some were praying to a God they didn't even know."

At the most desperate of moments, they cried out.

They believed he was there.

But they didn't know him.

GET ON YOUR KNEES

Studio 60 on the Sunset Strip was the short-lived follow-up show to Aaron Sorkin's successful television political drama, *West Wing*. *Studio 60* was a behind-the-scenes story of a late-night, sketch-comedy show (think *Saturday Night Live*).

The Harriet Hayes character, played by Sarah Paulson, is a Christian who works in a very secular environment. In one episode, she joins her friend and producer Danny Tripp (Bradley Whitford) at the hospital. His girlfriend is very sick. She has just given birth to a premature baby that Danny plans to raise as his own, and now his girlfriend is suffering from complications. In addition, Danny's employee (and Harriet's fellow cast member) has just learned that his brother has been taken hostage in Iraq.

Harriet sees an opportunity and asks Danny if he'd like to learn how to pray. Danny agrees. The following scene takes place in the hospital chapel:

> **Harriet:** Get down on your knees.
> **Danny:** Really?
> **Harriet:** Yeah.
> **Danny:** Why?
> **Harriet:** Respect.
> **Danny:** See, this is my first speed bump. I would think if I were God, I wouldn't have any ego problems. I wouldn't need a "Lord, Creator of the Universe, Most Powerful and Merciful, and Handsome of all the deities." There is a baby that is two weeks premature. Her mom can't stop bleeding. My friend and employee's brother is being held prisoner by medieval heroin dealers. If he needs ten minutes of sucking up before he'll fix this, I don't want to work with him. [2]

In the first chapter, we talked about prayer as an intimate conversation with a friend, but in an effort to be helpful, well-intentioned Christians often worry more about the technique than the relationship. This is what tripped up Danny Tripp. Danny is authentic in his conversation. Emotionally desperate, he gets that he needs God, but what he doesn't get is why he has to stop and give God a spiritual ego-stroking before getting to the point.

Harriet tells Danny, "The kneeling isn't for Him. It's for you." For Harriet, being on her knees is a physical reminder of her position to God. And that works—for her. She has a relationship with God. The problem is that Danny doesn't.

Yet.

Like the Virginia Tech students, he is getting ready to pray to a God he doesn't know. For him, kneeling is getting in the way, not only of the prayer, but of getting to know God through prayer.

> **Danny:** If He's everything you say He is, I shouldn't have to audition—
> **Harriet:** It's not an audition.
> **Danny:** If He's real—
> **Harriet:** He is.
> **Danny:** And He loves me—
> **Harriet:** He does.
> **Danny:** Why not just fix it?

Isn't that what so many of us want to know?

Why doesn't God just fix it?

We don't want to *have* to use certain words, or a specific technique, when we pray to God; we just want him to take care of things. Danny gets something here that even Harriet doesn't get.

He gets that prayer doesn't work.

God works.

He realizes that it isn't about his knees; it's about God. But Harriet's counterpoint is that it is our position to God. She tells Danny kneeling isn't for God, but for him.

Danny: How is it for me?

Harriet: It takes the average person in America sixty years to make what you make in a year. It takes the average person in the world sixty lifetimes to earn what you earn in a year. You have choices, same is true for me, and the one thing that isn't handed to you on a silver platter is humility. So I like to begin each day on my knees and end each day on my knees.

As the conversation continues, Harriet again asks Danny to get on his knees. Danny is so frustrated that he can't contain it:

Danny: I wasn't handed anything on a platter, I am who I am because my parents gave me opportunities. I am who I am because I worked hard and got good grades. I got what I got because I went after a non-paying, entry-level television internship and proved myself. I got what I got because *I took action*.

But as Harriet reminds him, there are some things that are beyond him:

Harriet: Are you a surgeon or a hematologist?
Danny: No.
Harriet: Then what action can you take now?

Everyone Prays

For some of us, like Harriet, prayer is a daily habit. We do it the same way every day, almost without thinking.

For others, we do it in the dark. And we don't want to admit we do it.

Then there are those, like Danny, who are intellectually opposed to praying, yet become emotionally aroused to the idea when the situation is desperate. When life is out of control. That's what happened to the students inside that dorm room. And while Danny doesn't pray with Harriet, on her terms in the chapel, the episode ends with him kneeling in front of the hospital's nursery window.

When we come to the end of ourselves, instinctively we cry out to someone outside of ourselves.

We all pray.

Eventually.

But here's the thing,

if we're all going to pray . . .

if we're going to link ourselves together in some sort of celestial pact . . .

doesn't it make sense to know who we're linking to?

We get references on plumbers, real estate agents, and painters. We do more to investigate doctors who represent our temporal bodies than the deity who heals our eternal spirits. If we're entering into relationship with the Divine— and every time we pray, we are—doesn't it make sense to have some divine understanding?

Just as it behooves the prisoner to make friends with the jailer or the line worker to make friends with the shift supervisor, it only makes sense for us to be in relationship with our Creator.

Does relationship ensure special consideration?

Yes.

It doesn't guarantee the outcome, but it certainly helps

with the process of asking. When we are in relationship with someone, we have knowledge about them. We know what they like, what they don't like, and how they like to do business. Whether it's being able to read the jailer's moods, timing a request for a raise from the boss, or getting the car keys from a parent or a spouse, being in a relationship gives us an understanding about how things work.

And how to make them work for us.

Imagine what it's like to be in a relationship with the Creator of the universe.

When we know God—it's like getting the secrets of the universe handed to us. Could it be that prayer is the conduit to that knowledge?

Prayerful conversation is a way to connect with an invisible God. Through prayer we learn about his desires, how things work, and how best to approach him. Prayer is the equivalent of having a few drinks with the boss after work. It doesn't ensure favor, but it ensures face time.

And God, in turn, works through prayer.

After all, it only takes one answered prayer, "Are you there, God?" to be assured that he's there and he's interested in a relationship with us. Answered prayer is one way God proves his presence.

But answered prayers are not replicable. We can't pick a few verses from the Bible, throw salt over our shoulder, or rub beads and demand a specific result. Even if it happens, causation can't be proved. Science and anecdotal evidence can convince us that prayers are both answered and not answered.

Did the patient live because his wife prayed, or because the antibiotic worked?

Did the marriage survive because God intervened, or because the couple went to counseling?

Did the clouds part and the rainbow come out because it was a sign, or because that's how weather phenomena work?

Perhaps questioning the answer is the wrong question.

Perhaps we should ask what's behind the answer.

When we pray, we're boldly asking to connect with the Master of the universe, to enter into a relationship with him. The mechanism that works in prayer is relational. We connect with God, and he touches the fever of the child—the answer we get is God's face, not merely his hand.

He teases and woos us into relationship by putting us in a wild, beautiful, uncontrollable world that we can't make work without him, no matter how hard we try. This explains both why life is so hard and why we consciously and even unconsciously feel compelled to cry out to him when we feel out of control.

People who are in desperate situations will do things they wouldn't normally do—even pray. Therefore, we should understand that our desperate pleas are asking for more than answers, more than changes to our circumstances, and more than specific transactions. Our primal prayers ask for relationship with the Creator of the universe, and it is in that *relationship* that we find the answers we are looking for.

When we pray, we're asking for God. This is what he wants too. If we feel like our prayers aren't being answered, perhaps it is because we don't see the answers. We don't recognize God's responses. The way to correct that is not to learn better techniques, but to learn more about God.

The benefit is that when we're in a relationship with God, we also learn more about ourselves.

GOD IS RELATIONSHIP

Yes, God likes relationships. And yes, he desires one with us. But it's more than that. God *is* a relationship. He is three-in-one, Father, Son, and Holy Spirit. (And it gets even more confusing.) Scholars and theologians more knowledgeable than your authors have made the subject completely incomprehensible, so we won't frost that cake. But you don't even have to lick a beater to understand that three-in-one is some sort of *community*.

God, by himself, is a community. He is in relationship with himself. And he created us in his image. Perhaps that explains the longings we have, our desires to be completed in a way that even a spouse can't complete us. We need that kind of inexplicable closeness, and where we find it is in relationship with God.

IN RELATIONSHIP WE CAN HAVE ANYTHING

Could it be that when we pray, we ask for stuff?

Material stuff,

stuff to happen,

or stuff to be different?

But perhaps God's first answer to our prayers is a question.

"Is this really what you want?"

Like any father, he wants us to have the stuff we need and the stuff we desire. But like a good father, he also knows that sometimes the stuff we ask for isn't the stuff we really want or need.

When Jordan and his dad were in New York City, they stopped by an art gallery that specialized in work by internationally renowned 3-D pop artist Charles Fazzino. They were looking for a specific piece they had seen during a previous trip, and when they found it still hanging in the gallery, they tried not to drool.

The piece was titled *In a Yankee State of Mind* and it featured not only the soon-to-be-demolished Yankee Stadium, but 3-D cutouts of eleven players, each with an autograph.

As the gallery salesman worked them over, their lust for the piece started to melt the promise they were "just going to look." Jordan kept saying, "Come on, Dad" each time the salesman made a point about the future value of the work increasing while he simultaneously decreased the walk-out price. And David wanted it; you could see it on his face. Pressure from the salesman. Pressure from his kid. And pressure from his own baseball-loving heart. But the thought of shelling out thousands of dollars kept him from committing.

Finally, he turned to Jordan and said, "You have a two-hundred-dollar gift card at home. Would you be willing to give that up, as well as your birthday and Christmas present for this year, if we bought this picture?" If Jordan said yes, the deal was done.

Jordan paused a mere two seconds and said, "Both Christmas and birthday? No way!"

Sometimes a good father knows that we're not really committed to getting what we're asking for.

Perhaps God is the same. He stops us and says, "Do you really want the stuff you're praying for? Because, as your

Father, I want you to have the stuff you need. And I'd love to give you the stuff you desire, but I think there's more than you know about, and I'd like to spend some time showing it to you."

That kind of transaction takes place during prayer.

Prayer is the actual time of connection. That is the time where God asks us questions and we respond. It's where relationship happens.

If our prayers are like bubbles, blown from our mouths by a breath of whim, only to pop when they land, we miss real conversation with God. But if our prayers are launched with the military precision of a rocket, sent straight to the heavens where they drop a satellite that continually beams our request, then these are the kinds of prayers God can't help but respond to. This is the stuff of which real relationships with God are made.

It's not the posture (kneeling or fasting or even chained to another monk) that carries our prayer to God's ear; it's the seriousness, the intentionality, with which we deliver it.

When God says to ask, he's saying *ask*.

Commit.

Boldly go forth and request.

A mini-revival took place in a subdivision in the South. There, an entire neighborhood prayed for a young father dying of cancer. His prognosis wasn't good, but the neighborhood rallied behind him and his family in prayer. These weren't casual, "when you think of it, remember Joe" kind of prayers. These were mothers crying at the supper table, saying, "It could be me. You've got to do something, God" kind of prayers. It was couples getting together and praying in the evenings. It was prayer beside mailboxes and chain-link fences. It was teenage prayer blasting from the stereo next door and dog prayers that barked all night. It was intercession at its finest.

As a result, several people in the neighborhood came to know Jesus.

To *yada* Jesus, as he *yada*'d them.

For many Christians, that would be enough. People prayed and came to know Jesus, so what more could you want? But the wife of the dying man wanted more. And for the praying people in that neighborhood it was more than the process. It was all about the answer. They wanted the man to live.

And he did.

He lived several more years, during which time he and his wife had another child.

Today, in that same neighborhood, there is a marriage that is strained beyond the bonds that once held it together. A man and wife are dealing with her infidelity and his jealousy. Neighbors gossip about how the kids are suffering from emotional trauma. But one woman, one mad, insanely desperate woman, is moved to prayer—the kind of prayer that spills over from her personal quiet time to every conversation she has. She pleads and begs with people to join her in praying for this marriage. She's stepped up her own prayers from "Help him not to go off the deep end when the inevitable divorce happens" to "God, it's going to take a freakin' miracle to keep this marriage together, but I am demanding you do it."

Her prayers, like those of Paul, the young U.S. Marine stationed in Iraq, are fierce, demanding, and audacious. If you knew the details of this marriage, you wouldn't be praying for it to be saved. But she is. She is storming the gates of heaven for a miracle.

These are the kinds of prayers that God answers.

Prayers that we're serious about.

Earnest prayers.

Prayers that boldly and faithfully demand action through relationship, not acquaintanceship.

Are your prayers for stuff being answered?

How badly do you want your stuff, and how badly do you want *his stuff*?

What are you willing to bargain your life away for?

What questions do you demand an answer to?

What "why?" are you going to turn into a "how?"

What injustice must stop?

What are you desperate to have God answer?

What is authentic and real about your prayers?

What prayer is so big you haven't yet dared to pray it?

When will you invite him into your deepest, boldest, and scariest prayers?

Situations may provoke us to prayer, but prayer provokes God to action. What will God do when provoked? Paul said in a letter to the Romans that God didn't spare even his Son:

> If God didn't hesitate to put everything on the line for us, embracing our condition and exposing himself to the worst by sending his own Son, is there anything else he wouldn't gladly and freely do for us? And who would dare tangle with God by messing with one of God's chosen? Who would dare even to point a finger? The One who died for us—who was raised to life for us!—is in the presence of God at this very moment

sticking up for us. Do you think anyone is going to be able to drive a wedge between us and Christ's love for us? There is no way![3]

Prayer is our connection with the Creator of the universe, who will always do what is best for us. God answers bargaining prayers, questioning prayers, prayers for justice, desperate prayers, audacious prayers, and prayers for beauty and happiness. But it's not just six prayers that he answers, or sixty—or six times sixty—but six-infinity prayers.

Life is hard, so we pray.

And he answers.

God is the ultimate golf pro. He wraps his arms around ours and helps us to hit the ball harder, farther, and with better aim than we can on our own, but he only does this through the invitation of prayer.

We have to let him in.

To know us.

To *yada* us.

And to know and *yada* him.

Prayer doesn't work. God works.

And God works when people pray.

NOTES

Chapter 1

1. Benjamin Franklin, "Constitutional Convention Address on Prayer" (Philadelphia, June 28, 1787), www.americanrhetoric.com/speeches/benfranklin.htm.

2. R. C. Sproul, "Chained Together for 12 Centuries," *Mission Gate Prison Ministry*, www.charityadvantage.com/missiongateministry/images/Acts7.doc.

3. Brendan O'Neill, "'New hedonism': flipside to fear," *spiked*, December 28, 2001, www.spiked-online.com/Articles/00000002D381.htm; James Joyner, "South Korean Condom Sales Rise After North Korean Nuke Test," *Outside the Beltway*, October 26, 2006, www.outsidethebeltway.com/archives/2006/10/south_korean_condom_sales_rise_after_north_korean_nuke_test.

4. Paul Davenport, "New Government Statistics on China's Christians," Compass Direct News Service (2000), www.worthynews.com/news-features/compass-china-survey.html.

5. Heidi Broadhead, "Billy Collins at The Poetry Center" (2001), www.poetrycenter.org/involved/news/collins.html.

Chapter 2

1. Luke 11:9, NIV.

2. John 14:13, NLT.

3. Miriam Schulman, "The Bargain," *Makkula Center for Applied Ethics*, www.scu.edu/ethics/publications/iie/v14n1/bargain.html.

4. "The Civil War: The Emancipation Proclamation," *Digital History*, www.digitalhistory.uh.edu/database/article_display.cfm?HHID=104.

5. Abraham Lincoln, "The Emancipation Proclamation" (Washington, D.C., January 1, 1863), www.archives.gov/exhibits/featured_documents/emancipation_proclamation/transcript.html.

6. Matthew 20:1-15, authors' paraphrase.

7. Barbara R. Bodengraven, "From Infantry to Seminary," *Light & Life*, Summer 2006, www.wjst.edu/File/Summer_L_L_2006.pdf.

8. Genesis 18:24-33, authors' paraphrase.

9. Victor A. Korniejczuk, "Psychological Theories of Religious Development: A Seventh-Day Adventist Perspective" (paper prepared for the International Faith and Learning Seminar, Union College, Lincoln, NB, June 1993), www.aiias.edu/ict/vol_10/10cc_257-276.htm.

10. See Matthew 18:3.

11. "Martin Luther: The Tower Experience, 1519," *Internet Modern History Sourcebook*, www.fordham.edu/halsall/mod/1519luther-tower.html.

Chapter 3

1. James Simpson, "SETI Allen Telescope Array in northern California set up to search for ET," www.earthtimes.org/articles/show/3012.html.

2. Ariana Eunjung Cha, "Finding Support in Search for E.T.," *Washington Post*, May 30, 2005, www.washingtonpost.com/wp-dyn/content/article/2005/05/29/AR2005052900966_pf.html.

3. "Pascal's Wager," *Stanford Encyclopedia of Philosophy*, http://plato.stanford.edu/entries/pascal-wager/.

4. You can find this story in 1 Kings 19.

5. See Philippians 2:5-8.

6. Matthew 27:46, NIV.

7. "I Believe," www.christians.org/creed/creed02.html.

Chapter 4

1. "Butterfly effect," *Wikipedia*, http://en.wikipedia.org/wiki/Butterfly_effect; "Cooking with Chaos," *InTute*, www.intute.ac.uk/sciences/spotlight/issue13/chaos.html.

2. "Butterfly effect," *Wikipedia*, http://en.wikipedia.org/wiki/Butterfly_effect.

3. See John 3:1-16.

4. Job 42:1-6, *The Message*.

5. Ibid.

6. See, for example Exodus 20:5, Proverbs 23:29-33, Genesis 12:17, 2 Samuel 12:15.

7. We've paraphrased the story but you can read more in John 9.

8. Psalm 62:11-12, NIV.

9. Luke 4:18-19.

10. "Why Children Ask 'Why'," *Dr.Greene.com*, www.drgreene.org/body.cfm ?id=21&action=detail&ref=564.

Chapter 5

1. See Romans 2:15.

2. Jeremiah 12:1.

3. Amos 5:24.

4. See Matthew 21:18-19.

5. Psalm 139:19.

6. Psalm 31:17.

7. Aaron Cahall, "In a rush? Sidewalk rage drives pedestrians off the deep end," Columbia News Service, http://jscms.jrn.columbia.edu/cns/2007-03-13/cahall-sidewalkrage.

8. *The Merchant of Venice*, Act 3 Scene 1.

9. www.coolquotes.com/quotes/albert_schweitzer.html.

10. Psalm 9:16.

11. Psalm 11:7.

12. Deuteronomy 32:4.

13. Isaiah 30:18, NIV.

14. Deuteronomy 32:41.

15. Abraham J. Heschel, *The Prophets* (New York: Harper & Row, 1962), 253, 276.

16. Gary A. Haugen, *Good News About Injustice* (Downers Grove, IL: InterVarsity, 1999), 80.

17. Ibid., 81.

18. Read about it in Luke 18:1-8.

19. Matthew 18:23-35, authors' paraphrase.

20. Linda Thomson, "Mother of shooting victim forgives killer, *Deseret Morning News*, March 12, 2007, http://deseretnews.com/dn/view/0,1249,660202106,00.html.

21. See Romans 12:19.

Chapter 6

1. http://sci.rutgers.edu/forum/showthread.php?t=51497

2. Transcribed from the documentary film *The Last Days* (October Films, 1989). Directed amd edited by James Moll.

3. www.healthtouch.com/bin/EContent_HT/cnoteShowLfts.asp?fname= 02180&title=RIB+FRACTURE+&cid=HTHLTH; www.sneezing-specifics. info/Sneezing-aneurysm.html.

4. "Bottled Water: Pure Drink or Pure Hype?" *Natural Resources Defense Council*, www.nrdc.org/water/drinking/nbw.asp.

5. "Estimating Population Size: Mark-Recapture," (lab assignment for BIOL 3113 Spring 2004), www.bio.georgiasouthern.edu/bio-home/leege/markrecapture.html.

6. "Demodex," *Wikipedia*, http://en.wikipedia.org/wiki/Demodex_mite.

7. "GMAC Insurance Study: Some 20 Million Drivers are Potential Accidents Waiting to Happen," *Insurance Journal*, May 26, 2005, www.insurancejournal.com/news/national/2005/05/26/55472.htm.

8. "Facts about Drowning," *The City of West Covina*, www.westcov.org/kids/drown.html.

9. Ricki Lewis, "The Rise of Antibiotic-Resistant Infections," *FDA Consumer*, September 1995, www.fda.gov/Fdac/features/795_antibio.html.

10. Luca Bucchini and Lynn R. Goldman, "Starlink Corn: A Risk Analysis," *Environmental Health Perspectives*, 110.1 (2002), www.ehponline.org/members/2002/110p5-13bucchini/bucchini-full.html.

11. "History of Rabbits in Australia," *Feral Feast*, http://library.thinkquest.org/03oct/00128/en/rabbits/history.htm.

12. "Organized Crime," *Encyclopaedia Britannica Online*, www.britannica.com/eb/topic-432090/organized-crime.

13. William Tucker, "Rent control drives out affordable housing," *USA Today*, July 1, 1998, www.encyclopedia.com/doc/1G1-20954302.html.

14. "Murphy's Laws Origin," *Murphy's Laws Site*, www.murphys-laws.com/murphy/murphy-true.html.

15. "Dunkirk," www.bbc.co.uk/weather/features/dunkirk.shtml.

16. Charles Simpson, pastoral letter, November 2001, http://www.csmpublishing.org/pastoral_full.php?pastoral=34.

17. Psalm 60:1-2.

18. Mark 5:28.

19. Mark 1:40 NIV.

20. Mark 1:41, NIV.

21. See John 11:14-15.

22. Transcribed from *The Last Days*.

23. "A Study Guide Based on the File . . . *The Last Days*," copyright © 1999–2000 by Survivors of the Shoah Visual History Foundation, 14.

24. Ibid.

25. Shayna Richardson, interview by Hannah Storm, *The Early Show*, CBS, December 13, 2005, www.cbsnews.com/stories/2005/12/13/earlyshow/main1120132.shtml.

26. Ibid.

Chapter 7

1. David Berkowitz, "My Story" (1999), www.forgivenforlife.com/
   1a-testimony.html.

2. J. R. R. Tolkien, *The Lord of the Rings*, book 1, *The Fellowship of the
   Ring* (Great Britain: HarperCollins, 1994), 167.

3. See Luke 18:9-14.

4. "Tortured Souls," *Boston Legal* episode, 2005, www.imdb.com/title/
   tt0530537/quotes.

5. Reuters, "Students admit to cheating but are they telling the truth?"
   June 7, 2007, www.reuters.com/article/lifestyleMolt/
   idUSN0637843420070607.

6. Nick Schager, "Marjoe," *Slant*, 2006, www.slantmagazine.com/film/film_
   review.asp?ID=2012.

7. 1 Samuel 13, authors' paraphrase.

8. 1 Samuel 16:7, authors' paraphrase.

9. Psalm 63:1.

10. Read about it in Psalm 51:2-4, 9-12.

11. See 1 Samuel 16:13-14.

12. Matthew 6:5-7.

13. Mike McLoughlin, "A Cry for Authentic Christian Living," *Mike
    McLoughlin's Blog*, January 3, 2005, http://blog.mike.mcloughlin.com/
    blog/_archives/2005/1/3/223092.html.

14. Julia Baird, "BeliefWatch: Got Faith?" *Newsweek* online, www.
    newsweek.com/id/33138.

15. Luke 6:41.

16. Chuck Colson, "Son of Sam, Child of God," *Breakpoint*, September 2,
    1999, www.breakpoint.org/listingarticle.asp?ID=2964.

Chapter 8

1. Transcribed from "Catalyst Preview—Donald Miller.m4v" on www.
   catalystspace.com, September 2006. This video is apparently no longer
   accessible online.

2. "Bart Gets an F," *The Simpsons*, http://www.snpp.com/episodes/7F03.
   html.

3. Ibid.

4. Luke 11:5-8, authors' paraphrase.

5. Luke 18:1-5, authors' paraphrase.

6. Mark 11:23-24, authors' paraphrase.

7. Matthew 7:7-8, authors' paraphrase.

8. Matthew 17:20, authors' paraphrase.

9. John 14:12-13, authors' paraphrase.
10. John 15:7, authors' paraphrase.
11. Matthew 21:22, authors' paraphrase.
12. I John 5:14-15, authors' paraphrase.
13. Matthew 17:21, authors' paraphrase.
14. R. B. Byrd "Positive therapeutic effects of intercessory prayer in a coronary care unit population," *Southern Medical Journal* 81:826–829.
15. See Luke 11:11-12.
16. C. S. Lewis, *The Weight of Glory: And Other Addresses* (San Francisco: Harper, 2001), 26.
17. "Catalyst Preview"
18. Mark 9:35, authors' paraphrase.

Chapter 9

1. Stendhal, *Love*, Gilbert and Suzanne Sale, trans. (New York: Penguin, 1975), 66.
2. G. K. Chesteron, *Orthodoxy* (Orlando: Relevant, 2006), 44.
3. See John 2:1-11.
4. See Matthew 17
5. See Romans 1:25.
6. W. Somerset Maugham, *Cakes and Ale* (Garden City, NY: Doubleday Doran, 1930), 140.

Chapter 10

1. "If You Love Something," *John Mark Ministries*, http://jmm.aaa.net.au/articles/7729.htm.
2. "If You Love Something," *Giggles & Laughs*,www.inspiredliving.com/humor/humor_IfYouLove.htm.
3. "You Know How They Say If You Love Something Let It Go?" *Yahoo! Answers*, http://answers.yahoo.com/question/index?qid=20070526142826AALUYFv&show=7.
4. Jeremiah 1:5, NIV.
5. See Mark 5:4.
6. Mark 5:15.
7. Read about it in Mark 10:1-29.
8. J. D. Schultz and J. G. West, eds.,*The C. S. Lewis Readers Encyclopedia.* (Grand Rapids, MI: Zondervan, 1998).
9. See Hebrews 12:6
10. Colossians 4:17.
11. Read about this in Exodus 4.

12. See Judges 6.
13. See Matthew 18.
14. Graham Greene, *The End of the Affair,* Penguin second U.S. edition (New York: Penguin, 1999), 192.
15. Matthew 7:7.
16. Matthew 7:21-23.
17. Revelation 3:20.

Chapter 11

1. "Some Were Praying to a God They Didn't Even Know," *Christian Index*, April 26, 2007.
2. "K&R Part I; K&R Part II; K&R Part III." *Studio 60 on the Sunset Strip—Complete Series*, DVD (2006; Burbank, CA; Warner Home Video, 2007).
3. Romans 8:31-39, *The Message*

An Acknowledgment of Prayers Already Answered

We DON'T THINK IT'S an accident that you're reading this book. We believe that God used many people to help connect you with the ideas that are in these pages. We'd like to take a minute to thank as many of them as we can.

The authors first met at the 2005 Write to Publish Conference (www.writetopublish.com) in Wheaton, Illinois. Because of Lin Johnson's commitment to train writers, and her excellent organizational skills, the authors first connected over words and ideas in a late-night owl session. Over the next three days (and then the next three years), we came to realize what a divine appointment that was.

Beth Jusino of Alive Communications recognized the strategic importance of this writing partnership long before we did. She advised, guided, and counseled us years before she represented us. For her time, attention to details, strategic counsel, and most of all her friendship, we are eternally grateful.

Ken Petersen asked all the right questions over dinner at the Macaroni Grill. He was the genesis of the idea that became this book. Without his counsel and guidance, this book would literally (and figuratively) not exist. Though he has moved on to other things, his brilliant fingerprints are on every page. Thanks also to Jon Wilcox, who was at that dinner and provided early feedback to our ideas.

Carol Traver stepped into a project that wasn't hers and made it her own. We can't imagine having been blessed with a more enthusiastic editor. She is wise counsel with a stand-up-comedian delivery. Her loyalty to her authors is unparalleled.

We are so appreciative of the support we've received at Tyndale from Ron Beers, Carla Mayer, Maria Eriksen, and Vicki Lynch. Dave Lindstedt made us sound like better writers than we are. There are others we have yet to meet in editorial, graphics, sales and marketing, publicity, and elsewhere. We thank you for what you've done and for what you are yet to do. We are truly *honored* to be working with such a fine company and alongside such quality people. In the summer of 2006, before this book was even a thought, we sat in the Wendy's parking lot and prayed over your building and the people in it—that God would bless each one of you. Little did we know at the time that through you he would also bless us.

Many ideas that found their way into this book started with casual conversations with Patrick Borders, Sean Gaffney, Sharon Knudson, Jim Krueger, Pete Loescher, and Andre Riedlinger.

We are fortunate to have had so many early readers who invested hours reading, asking questions, and telling us hard truths. To Patrick Borders, Debbi Jo Dieter, Sean Gaffney, Julie Garmon, Elisabeth Herringshaw, Emily Herringshaw, DeAnn Lancashire, Tim McMahan, Jonathan Munson, Nan Thorten-Snipes, Brent Sweitzer, and Peter Watkins, we thank you for your time and excellent feedback.

266

Marlene Dickinson and Wayne Holmes provided considerable detailed comments that strengthened the manuscript. Teisha Moseley provided feedback, editorial assistance, and encouragement through *every* draft of the book. The book is better because of their assistance.

Our children, Emily, Elisabeth, Matthew, and Michael Herringshaw and Jordan Schuchmann, were patient while we were writing. Thank you for letting us tell your stories. Our spouses, Jill Herringshaw and David Schuchmann, were understanding, supportive, and encouraging throughout the process. Thank you for the grace you extended that we didn't deserve. We love each of you more than you'll ever know.

Though good content and good writing are the authors' responsibility, books happen because of a whole bunch of people who do their jobs without recognition: printers, loading-dock supervisors, truckers, book buyers, bookstore owners, salespeople, and even the janitors who dust the shelves after the stores close. Critics, interviewers, newspapers and magazines that still review books, bloggers, librarians, and booksellers work to connect books and readers. We don't know you by name, but we thank you for the connections you make every day on our behalf.

The ideas in this book didn't just happen; they were brought to you through a series of divine circumstances directed by our Creator. Do with them what you will. Our prayer is that they will glorify him who brought us together.

Without God's involvement, prayers are nothing more than hope-filled recitations. With his involvement, prayers are always answered.

—Mark and Jennifer

ABOUT THe AUTHOrS

Mark Herringshaw, Ph.D. serves as a teaching pastor of the 7,000 member North Heights Lutheran Church in Roseville, Minnesota. He is also professor of leadership at the Master's Institute Seminary in St. Paul and an accomplished writer, speaker, and seminar leader. His articles have appeared in such publications as *Alive!*, *In Touch*, and *Lutheran Renewal*.

Mark received a B.A. in biblical literature and English from Azusa Pacific University. He did graduate studies at Regent College, Luther Seminary, and Regent University before earning his Ph.D. from Regent University in 2001. He is the founder and director of eEmbassy, an organization that develops interactive educational experiences for youth, families, and the business community.

Mark has been married to Jill for twenty-two years. They have four children and live in Minnesota.

Jennifer Schuchmann, an award-winning writer, has published hundreds of articles in publications such as *Today's*

Christian, Marriage Partnership, Christian Parenting, Your Church, and *The Christian Communicator.* Her first book, *Your Unforgettable Life: Only You Can Choose the Legacy You Leave,* co-authored with Craig Chapin, was published by Beacon Hill in 2005.

She has also ghostwritten a book for an international leadership consultant, and has contributed to several other books, including *The Church Leader's Answer Book* (Tyndale, 2006), *Whispering in God's Ear* (WaterBrook, 2005), and a couples study Bible published by Zondervan (2007).

Jennifer holds an MBA from Emory University, with an emphasis in marketing and communications, and a bachelor's degree in psychology from the University of Memphis.

She and her husband, David, live in Georgia with their twelve-year-old son.

Coming Spring 2009

Mark Herringshaw &
Jennifer Schuchmann

nine
ways
GOD
ALways
speaks

Turn the page for a
Sneak Preview.

1
Hearing voices

Some things are too good to be true:

- living to be 101
- winning the lottery
- hearing God speak

Even though these things are out of the ordinary, and perhaps even unlikely, they do happen every day to people all over the world. With a healthy diet, exercise, and regular checkups you can outlast your genes. Buy enough scratch-off tickets and eventually you'll get lucky. But hearing God speak? Is there anything you can do about that?

We think so.

And so do others.

Many others.

CRAZY TALK

Perhaps God has spoken to you in the past and you'd like to experience that kind of communication again.

Maybe you've never heard from God personally—but you long to.

Or could it be that you are skeptical that God speaks at all?

One reason people say they don't pray more is that they feel as if nothing happens when they pray—that God isn't listening; or worse, that he's not there at all.

A one-sided relationship isn't much fun.

If we're expected to talk to God through prayer, shouldn't we at least know whether he will talk back?

When Jennifer was a high school sophomore, she was actively investigating the claims of Christianity but hadn't yet made a decision about their authenticity. While riding in a car with a guy from school, she had a very disturbing conversation, so disturbing that twenty years later she can still remember how nervous it made her. The guy was smart and cute, and Jennifer had a crush on him. Oh, and he was a Christian. Though cute and smart were good boyfriend traits, she wasn't so sure about the Christian part, especially when the guy happened to mention that God spoke to him.

> We were driving and talking. I don't remember the exact conversation, but I clearly remember he said, "God told me . . ." and all I could think was, *This guy must be crazy.* And I didn't mean crazy in some fun-loving way; I meant certifiably deranged. People who hear God's voice do crazy-people things like shoot their mothers or drown their kids in the bathtub.

I have to admit that I was nervous riding in a car with someone who thought he was hearing God speak, but like I said, he was cute. So I asked him about it.

"God speaks to you?"

"Yes."

"Do you hear voices? Is it like a deep voice, like in the movies?"

"No, not really—"

"Well, what does his voice sound like?"

"Well, it's kind of—"

"Wait. Do other people hear him when he speaks to you?" (I wasn't sure how I wanted him to answer that question.)

If God spoke only to him and no one else heard God's voice, then this guy was not boyfriend material; he was drown-our-future-kids material.

But if he said that other people also heard God speak to him—like eavesdropping on a conversation at a restaurant, where Cute Guy and God are discussing football scores—then it was even weirder.

Who else heard him? Was this guy a member of some strange cult? Or was it possible that God really did speak, and that he was speaking to everyone else, except me?

Fortunately, Cute Guy interrupted my thoughts with an explanation.

"No, it's not like God says things out loud to me, like Charlton Heston on a megaphone. It's more like it's a passing thought that comes into my head out of nowhere. It's more like a feeling than an audible voice."

"Then how do you know it's God?"

He patiently responded, and I kept peppering him with more questions about what he heard, how he heard it, what he'd had for dinner the night before he heard the voices, and whether he was taking any prescription drugs.

I left that conversation a little less skeptical and a lot more curious. If God really spoke to people, why wasn't he speaking to me? And how could I get him to start?

I finally decided that I couldn't believe it based on somebody else's report. If God wanted me to believe that he spoke to people, he'd have to speak to me personally.

Perhaps your story is similar to Jennifer's. You don't believe that God communicates with people on earth. Or maybe just the idea that the God of the universe might talk to you creeps you out. Maybe you don't even believe that God exists—let alone that he speaks.

Or could it be that you have a great deal of head knowledge about how God communicates, but not much in the way of personal experience? Perhaps you've grown up in the church or around religious folks who discussed how God communicates with man, but you're not convinced that he talks to you.

Perhaps you're chuckling as you read this because you know that God speaks and that he speaks to you personally. But maybe your expectations of how and when he speaks are limited by your experience.

Regardless of your story, your preconceived ideas, even

your experiences, what if much of what you think about God communicating with you is wrong?

What if there's a whole lot more to it than what you've seen so far?

What if God does speak?

What if he's speaking right now?